COMPOSING
SACRED SCRIPTURE

HOW THE BIBLE WAS FORMED

DONALD SENIOR, CP

LITURGY
TRAINING
PUBLICATIONS

Nihil Obstat
Very Reverend Daniel A. Smilanic, JCD
Vicar for Canonical Services
Archdiocese of Chicago
February 16, 2016

Imprimatur
Very Reverend Ronald A. Hicks
Vicar General
Archdiocese of Chicago
February 16, 2016

The *Nihil Obstat* and *Imprimatur* are declarations that the material is free from doctrinal or moral error, and thus is granted permission to publish in accordance with c. 827. No legal responsibility is assumed by the grant of this permission. No implication is contained herein that those who have granted the *Nihil Obstat* and *Imprimatur* agree with the content, opinions, or statements expressed.

COMPOSING SACRED SCRIPTURE: HOW THE BIBLE WAS FORMED © 2016 Archdiocese of Chicago: Liturgy Training Publications, 3949 South Racine Avenue, Chicago IL 60609, 1-800-933-1800; fax 1-800-933-7094; e-mail: orders @ltp.org; website: www.LTP.org. All rights reserved.

This book was edited by Lorie Simmons. Victor R. Perez was the production editor, Anna Manhart was the series designer, and Kari Nicholls was the production artist and cover designer.

Cover image is a reproduction of the Evangelist Matthew page from the Canterbury Codex Aureus, an illuminated manuscript of the eighth century located in the Kungliga Library in Stockholm. The Yorck Project, Wikimedia Commons.

Image on page viii from the Codex Sinaiticus, Wikimedia Commons.

20 19 18 17 16   1 2 3 4 5

Printed in the United States of America.

Library of Congress Control Number: 2016934237

ISBN 978-1-61671-272-3

LBCSS

Composing Sacred Scripture offers the work of a first-class scholar at his pastoral best. In clear, concise, nontechnical language, Donald Senior not only describes how the Bible was formed, but crystallizes essential content and characteristics of the New Testament books, especially the Gospels. Firmly rooted in scholarship and Church teaching, the author clarifies Catholic perspectives on the inspiration and truth of the Scriptures as the Word of God. A small gem with many facets!

—Marielle Frigge, OSB,
Professor Emerita, Religious Studies, Mount Marty College;
Director of Ongoing Formation,
Sacred Heart Monastery, Yankton, South Dakota

In the hands of a wise and venerable teacher, readers of this book will greatly enrich their comprehension of the Bible. Written for beginning students in a style that's inviting and accessible, this short volume will whet appetites for further study and nurture love and understanding of Scripture. Particularly recommended for proclaimers of the Word.

—Graziano Marcheschi, MA, DMIN,
Vice President for Mission and Ministry,
Saint Xavier University, Chicago

Well-known New Testament scholar Donald Senior, CP, has written a succinct, much-needed introductory book on the formation of the Bible. It is an ideal guide for everyone who desires a Catholic understanding of the Bible—especially readers and others serving in liturgical ministry, as well as catechists, teachers, and leaders of Bible study groups.

—Daniel J. Scholz, Associate Professor of Biblical Studies,
Cardinal Stritch University, Milwaukee, Wisconsin

Fr. Senior's book can give lectors and readers fresh energy for proclaiming the Word at Mass. Through the book's description of the historical periods, circumstances, and arenas in which the books of the Bible were written and compiled and its helpful explanation of the way God's Word is revealed through human words, lectors can gain a fresh perspective on the readings. The new knowledge provided by this book will complement their spiritual preparations and help them proclaim the Scriptures with more understanding and vigor.

—George Miller, Reader, Trainer,
and Founder of LectorResources.com

This work is dedicated to

Fr. Roger Mercurio, CP,
Fr. Barnabas Ahern, CP,
and Fr. Carroll Stuhlmueller, CP

—three great biblical scholars, teachers, and
mentors, to whom I will be forever grateful.

CONTENTS

Page from the fourth-century Greek Bible called Codex Sinaiticus ("the Sinai Book") showing the text of Matthew 2:5—3:7.

For more information about this book, see http://codexsinaiticus.org/en/, a collaboration of the British Library, the Library of the University of Leipzig, the National Library of Russia in St. Petersburg, and the Holy Monastery of the God-Trodden Mount Sinai (Saint Catherine's).

Getting Started

This book on the formation of the Bible is addressed to all those who love the Scriptures and to those also who open the beauty and power of the Bible for others; for example, those who serve in the ministry of the Word: readers, psalmists, liturgists, catechists, Bible study group leaders, teachers, and preachers. It will also serve those who study the Scriptures to deepen their knowledge of their faith heritage and to nourish their own spiritual lives.

This book is not a commentary on Scripture or a standard introduction to the Scriptures; there are plenty of such resources available today. Rather it is a study of how the Bible came into existence and of the makeup of what we call our Sacred Scriptures. Knowing more about the formation of the Bible can enable us to be more alert to its message. The more we know about a person we love and treasure, the better we can appreciate them. Thus the purpose of this book is not simply academic or abstract—that is, to present the fruits of scholarship only for the sake of conveying knowledge about an important historical and cultural artifact—but to offer some insights about the formation and makeup of the Bible for those who love it and want to become more familiar with it for the sake of their own Christian faith.

Two Perspectives: Reason and Faith

Understanding how the Bible was formed can be viewed from two different but intimately related perspectives. On the one hand we can view the formation of the Bible from a historical and literary point of view, using our faculties of human reasoning. Virtually everyone who knows anything about the Bible realizes that it is not a single book written at one point in time but a collection of many books written over a long and complex historical period. Thus the historical perspective asks, how and when did the various books of the Bible originate? And at what point did these diverse components come together into one Bible? Similarly, it is clear that the Bible contains a wide variety of literary forms such as narratives and law codes and letters. Why and how did such a variety of literary forms make their way into the Bible? And what demands do these various literary forms place upon a proper reading and interpretation of the Bible?

On the other hand, for those who view the Bible from the vantage point of faith, there is another way of looking at the formation of the Bible. How did the Bible come to be seen as the "Word of God"? And why were these particular books of the Bible considered inspired and sacred while other apparently worthy candidates were not included?

These two perspectives should not be seen as opposed to each other. Those who may view the Bible solely as an important historical and cultural artifact, one that has had a profound impact on Western culture and beyond, will focus primarily on the first dimension, the historical and literary aspects. But those who view the Bible as their Sacred Scriptures cannot be content simply with viewing the Bible from a historical and literary point of view. The role of the Scriptures within Judaism (that is, what Christians consider the Old Testament) or from the vantage point of Christian faith (that is, both the Old and New Testaments) involves profound and challenging theological issues. Here the question becomes: How does the formation of the Bible illumine and support the belief in the Bible as God's inspired Word? Both perspectives are necessary for a complete understanding of the Bible. To study the Bible simply from a historical or literary point of view overlooks the meaning of the Bible for communities of faith—primarily Judaism and Christianity—which have faithfully carried the Bible through history and been nourished by it. On the other hand, to focus solely on the explicitly religious or spiritual dimension of the Bible and to ignore its historical and literary character is to risk making the Bible some sort of "magical" book that dropped mysteriously from heaven and has no root within human history.

Catholic tradition has emphasized both dimensions of the Scriptures. The Bible is God's Word but also formed and composed in authentically human words. This was a firm teaching, for example, of the *Dogmatic Constitution on Divine Revelation (Dei Verbum,* 12), a document from the Second Vatican Council: "God speaks in sacred Scripture through men in human fashion." The text goes on to say that, therefore, interpreters of Scripture need to be attentive to its literary forms and historical context. In his 2010 Post-synodal Apostolic Exhortation, *Verbum Domini (The Word of the Lord),* Pope Benedict XVI makes a similar point in emphasizing that there should not be a cleavage between reason and faith in approaching the Scriptures.[1] Approaching the Scriptures from a purely rational point of view robs them of their ultimate meaning; approaching the Scriptures from a purely religious point of view can lead to distortion and a fundamentalist approach to biblical interpretation.

> The Bible is God's Word but also formed and composed in authentically human words.

The Role of Liturgy and Worship in the Formation of the Bible

In accord with the purpose of this Liturgy and the Bible series, we will give attention to the role of the liturgy in the formation of the Bible. In both the Old and the New Testament, worship and liturgical celebration were a prime incubator for the emergence of the biblical texts. At several key moments in the biblical saga we find descriptions in the Scriptures of the assembly of Israel worshipping God and remembering God's fidelity to his people. In the New Testament we can demonstrate how the Gospel accounts, Paul's letters, and other

---

1   *The Word of the Lord,* 36.

writings of the New Testament were proclaimed in the context of liturgy—particularly the Eucharist—and, in turn, were shaped by that liturgical context.

Understanding the importance of liturgy and worship in the formation of the Bible throws light on the ultimate purpose of the Scriptures—they lead us to glorify God.

The Formation of the Bible and the Catholic Biblical Movement

The ability to freely explore the historical, literary, and theological dimensions of the Scriptures from a Catholic perspective has been made possible by the remarkable transformation in Catholic biblical studies since the beginning of the twentieth century. The Bible has always had a central place in the worship and theology of the Church. The theological reflections of most of the patristic theologians of the early centuries of the Church took place in homilies centered on interpreting the biblical message. When Christianity came into its own in the Church that developed after Emperor Constantine in the early fourth century, when it could design its own houses of worship and publicly display its art, biblical motifs played a central role by communicating the biblical message to a largely illiterate audience. The liturgy and most popular devotions of the Church were also suffused with biblical motifs, narratives, and images. The great medieval theologians published much of their theology through commentaries on Scripture.

However, the advent of the Protestant Reformation in the sixteenth century, with its emphasis on Scripture as the sole criteria of judgment for authentic Christianity (*sola Scriptura*) and the use of Scripture as a means of critique for the perceived corruptions of the late medieval Church, set up a defensive reaction on the part of the Catholic Church. Church leaders were concerned about the faithful interpreting Scripture on their own, independent of Church guidance, and responded by emphasizing Church tradition and authority, thus tempering the access of ordinary Catholics to the Scriptures. The rise of the Enlightenment in the eighteenth century and its emphasis on the superiority of human reason and reliance on measurable, physical evidence in all matters made Church officials fear that such studies were motivated by a desire to rob the Scriptures—and religion itself—of their transcendent character. In many cases, that was true, but the reaction of many Catholic leaders was too comprehensive and led to a bitter suppression of Catholic biblical scholarship.

Such a reaction came to its climax in the late nineteenth and early twentieth centuries, culminating in Pope Pius X's condemnation of modernism. Catholic biblical scholars had to tread very lightly. A great figure such as Marie-Joseph LaGrange, OP, the founder of the École biblique, the prestigious graduate biblical school in Jerusalem, suffered constant oppression from Church officials. Forbidden to publish on biblical topics, he was pulled back for a time from his beloved Jerusalem to teach high school in France, and was constantly under suspicion, despite his deep piety and unwavering loyalty to the Church.[2]

Only over time, and in part because of their evident faith and devotion that proved not to be incompatible with vigorous historical inquiry, did such Catholic scholars quiet the fears and suspicion of Church officials. A particularly important breakthrough was the 1943 encyclical of Pope Pius XII, *Divino Afflante Spiritu*, considered the magna carta of modern Catholic biblical studies. The pope's encyclical was full of encouragement for biblical scholars, urging them to pursue their studies of the Scriptures without fear and utilizing the tools of linguistics, historical inquiry, literary forms, and the emerging results of archaeology. While expressing reverence for the Vulgate—that is, the

The 1943 encyclical of Pope Pius XII, *Divino Afflante Spiritu*, is considered the magna carta of modern Catholic biblical studies.

---

2   See Bernard Montagnes, OP , *The Story of Father Marie-Joseph Lagrange: Founder of the Modern Catholic Bible Study* (New York: Paulist Press, 2006).

traditional Latin translation of the Bible—the Pope also urged that new translations be made from the original biblical languages of Hebrew and Greek.

Pius XII's encyclical led to an explosion of biblical studies within the Catholic community, including the United States, where a whole generation of leading scholars such as Raymond Brown, SS, Joseph Fitzmyer, SJ, Roland Murphy, OCARM, and Carroll Stuhlmueller, CP, to name but a few, came on the scene. The surge in scholarship was matched with a growing interest in study of the Scriptures on the part of ordinary Catholics, an interest spurred as well by a similar awakening in the liturgical movement.

This renewed biblical movement helped prepare for the strong Scripture focus of the Second Vatican Council and one of its most important texts, the *Dogmatic Constitution on Divine Revelation* (*Dei Verbum*, November 18, 1965). A draft of this document was introduced at the very beginning of the Council, but its content was deemed inadequate by most of the council fathers. Pope John XXIII assigned it to a commission that would finally produce a vastly improved version approved at the final session of the Council in November, 1965.[3]

As we will note, *Dei Verbum* elaborated a full theology of revelation and the role of the Scriptures within it.[4] It fully accepted the human dimension of the Scriptures and, as Pope Pius XII had done, gave vigorous encouragement both to Catholic biblical scholarship and to the incorporation of the Bible into all facets of the Church's life: its liturgy, preaching, theology, teaching, and its popular devotional life.

Dei Verbum gave vigorous encouragement to Catholic biblical scholarship and to the incorporation of the Bible into all facets of the Church's lifes.

The strong biblical accent of the Second Vatican Council, and in particular the theology of revelation elaborated in *Dei Verbum*,

---

3   On the history of this process, see Ronald D. Witherup, *The Word of God at Vatican II: Exploring "Dei Verbum"* (Collegeville: Liturgical Press, 2014).

4   See below, pages 118–125.

continue to have a positive impact on Catholic teaching at the highest levels of the Church's authority. For example, the Pontifical Biblical Commission, which was first established by Pius X at the beginning of the twentieth century as a watchdog to ensure orthodoxy among Catholic biblical scholars, was transformed in the wake of the Council by Pope Paul VI to become a resource for the Pope and the Vatican in matters biblical. Several of its studies were approved by the Popes for dissemination to the entire Church, such as the *Instruction Concerning the Historical Truth of the Gospels* (1964), *The Interpretation of the Bible in the Church* (1993), *The Jewish People and Their Sacred Scriptures in the Christian Bible* (2001), *The Bible and Morality* (2008), and its most recent study, *The Inspiration and Truth of Sacred Scripture* (2014). Each of these official Catholic instructions on Scripture employs historical-critical and literary methods and each does so from a Catholic faith perspective.

This study of the composition of the Bible will proceed in that spirit, examining the historical and literary process that led to the formation of the Bible, but doing so from a spirit of faith in the Scriptures as the Word of God and as the "Church's book."

Finally, to share my own perspective, I was first introduced to a thorough study of the Scriptures as a Passionist seminarian. Even though our major seminary in those days was quite small compared to most, we were fortunate and blessed to have three eminent Scripture scholars as our professors—each of whom had begun their graduate studies under the inspiration of Pope Pius XII's *Divino Afflante Spiritu*. This modest attempt to capture the nature and spirit of the Bible they loved is dedicated to them: Fr. Roger Mercurio, CP; Fr. Barnabas Ahern, CP; and Fr. Carroll Stuhlmueller, CP.

CHAPTER 1

An Anatomy of the Bible

The word "Bible" comes from the Greek word *ta biblia* that literally means "the books." The alternate term "Scripture" derives from the Latin word *scriptura* or "writings." As the plural form of both these words implies, the Bible is not a single volume written by a single author but a collection of diverse books written by multiple authors, in varying historical and cultural circumstances, in many different formats or literary forms, and over a long period of time.

The Diversity of the Bible

There is no doubt that the Bible contains diverse books of varying literary forms. The seventy-three books of the Catholic Bible (forty-six in the Old Testament; twenty-seven in the New[1]) include dramatic narratives in both the Old and New Testament, love poetry such as that of the Song of Songs, the law codes of Leviticus, the Gospel accounts of the life of Jesus, the letters of Paul, an apparent homily or exhortation such as the "Letter" to the Hebrews, the dramatic apocalyptic symbols and scenarios in the Book of Revelation, and many more literary forms.

The temporal span of the events included in the covers of the Bible stretch from the very beginning of time in the creation accounts of Genesis, through the patriarchal period, which is set within an approximate time frame from 1900 BC to 1300 BC, and on into the centuries of Israel's history from roughly 1250 down to the time of the Maccabees and the Hasmonean dynasty in the century

---

1   As we will discuss, there are some variations in the number of books included on the part of Jewish, Catholic, Protestant, and Orthodox traditions. See chapter 8, pages 100–117.

before the birth of Christ. The New Testament itself encompasses most of the first century of the Christian era, with the life of Jesus, the mission of Paul, the expansion of the early Church's mission, and the assortment of letters and other texts that are roughly dated to the last quarter of the first century.

The Geography of the Bible

The geographical arena in which the biblical saga of the Old Testament mainly takes place is the small strip of land along the eastern shore of the Mediterranean that forms the land bridge between the ancient civilizations of Mesopotamia to the northeast and Egypt to the southwest. The geographical arena of the New Testament is more expansive. Jesus and his disciples operate for the most part in the area of ancient Israel (in New Testament terms, Judea, Samaria, and Galilee). The Gospel accounts do note some brief forays of Jesus and his disciples into the northern region of Tyre and Sidon (present-day Lebanon), as well as to the Decapolis, a mainly Gentile region on the eastern side of the Sea of Galilee. In the post-Resurrection era of the early Church, as the Christian mission to the world expands, so does its geographical reach. We read in Acts 11:19–20 that Christians scattered by the persecution that followed the martyrdom of Stephen reach Antioch in the north, at that time the third largest city in the Roman Empire. From there Paul, Barnabas, and other Christian missionaries move to the west, through Asia Minor, on to Macedonia and the Greek Peloponnese, and eventually to Rome itself. We also hear of Christians, such as the early missionary Apollos, coming from Alexandria in Egypt (Acts 18:24). Early in the Acts of the Apostles, Philip the Deacon encounters an Ethiopian eunuch on the road to Gaza (Acts 8:26–40), suggesting the spread of the Gospel into northern Africa. We know from the account of Paul's conversion (Acts 9:1–22) that there were already Christians in Damascus, Syria, and in his letter to the Romans (15:24) Paul tells of his desire to travel to Spain, at that time the farthest western reach of the Roman Empire.

Such a span of time and space, of course, involves cultural as well as chronological diversity. The time of the patriarchs fits into the nomadic and agrarian cultures of the ancient Middle East. The history of Israel, as portrayed in the Bible, shows contact with Egyptian culture, the Canaanite culture of its promised homeland, tragic encounters with Assyrian and Babylonian invaders, life in exile in Babylon, the dominance of Persian culture, the lingering influence of Hellenistic (Greek) culture in the wake of the conquest of Alexander the Great, the resulting political and cultural intrusion of Greek dynasties, first from the Ptolomies in Egypt, and then from the Seleucid dynasty in Syria, and finally, the strong hand of the Roman Empire that would enter the biblical stage some sixty years before the birth of Christ and be a constant presence to the end of the New Testament period.

Of all of these, what we can call "Greco-Roman" culture had a particularly strong influence on the Bible. The term "Greco-Roman" refers to the foundational role that Greek culture and language had in the Mediterranean world from the time of Alexander. The Roman Empire itself would absorb and expand Greek culture, retaining use of its language (alongside the Roman Latin) and many of its cultural values and practices. The Greek overlords who remained in the Middle East in the wake of Alexander's invasion brought to this region the heritage of Greek culture: the Greek language; a consciousness of the role of the city as an economic and cultural center; love of sports and the cult of the body (for example, the gymnasium, the race track); greater attention to the individual within the bounds of the community; and a history of art and theatre.

The influx of Greek culture into the biblical world probably had its greatest impact on the elite classes of Israel. Most Jews in biblical Israel, who lived their lives on a subsistence level in rural areas, would have only a glancing contact with Greek culture. However, beginning with the Babylonian exile of the sixth century BC, Jews were dispersed throughout the Mediterranean world in the wake of various invasions, a pattern that would continue down through the Roman period. These Jews, referred to as "diaspora" Jews, even as they remained faithful to their Jewish heritage, would ultimately be immersed in Greco-Roman culture, speaking Greek instead of Hebrew or Aramaic and influenced strongly by the assumptions and values of the surrounding dominant culture.

This cultural reality helps explain the significant role that Greek would play in the Bible itself. According to a traditional story, diaspora Jews living in Alexandria translated the Hebrew Bible into Greek. The project began with the Pentateuch (the first five books of the Bible), but later the entire Bible would be translated for the sake of Greek-speaking Jews living in the wider Mediterranean world. Begun roughly in 281 BC and completed around 100 BC, the Greek translation was named the "Septuagint" (from the Greek word for "seventy"), since according to the traditional story mentioned earlier, the translation work was entrusted to seventy scribes who worked independently, yet miraculously produced identical translations!

The Septuagint is significant because it gave access to the Scriptures for the Greek-speaking Jews of the Mediterranean world, and also because it served as the actual Bible for the Christians themselves, since most of them would be Greek speaking. Most, but not all, of the quotations of the Old Testament found in the New Testament writings would be drawn from the Septuagint.

A Collection or a Coherent Whole?

There is no doubt that the Bible is made up of many diverse parts, but is it fully accurate to call it a "collection"? The term "collection" might imply that the books of the Bible are relatively independent of each other, gathered together without any overarching motif or subject, like books on a collector's shelf. Understood this way, the term "collection" would not reflect the complex interrelationship among the books of the Bible.

To a certain degree the order of the books of the Bible is chrono-logical. For example, stories of the creation of the world begin the biblical saga, followed by the accounts of the early ancestors of Israel, then the sojourn in Egypt, the account of the Exodus and the ultimate conquest of the land, the rise of the monarchy, the period of exile, and finally the return to the land. But this general chronological framework has many detours along the way as the Old Testament turns to the various prophetic and wisdom books. In the New Testament, also, there is a general chronological formation beginning with the four Gospel accounts of the life of Jesus and the story of the founding and expansion of the Church. But then this chronological framework gives way to the letters of Paul and a diverse group of other writings. The order of the New Testament books returns to something of a chronological sequence by placing the Book of Revelation last, with its vision of the defeat of evil and the fulfillment of the world's God-given destiny. Thus to a certain extent the various books of the Bible are grouped along a general chronological framework and are not simply a "collection." However, the general chronological sequence of the biblical saga does not necessarily imply that the books were written in chronological order; for example, we should not assume that Genesis would be the oldest book of the Bible because it begins the biblical story, or that the Gospel accounts are older than Paul's letters because they come first in the New Testament sequence.

> The general chronological sequence of the biblical saga does not necessarily imply that the books were *written* in chronological order.

The interrelationship of the diverse biblical books has another deeper and more complex level. Many of the biblical books draw upon motifs and incidents articulated in earlier works and in many instances reinterpret these previous materials. The Book of Deuteronomy, the fifth book of the Pentateuch (a Greek term that literally means "five books"), recapitulates and reinterprets much of the previous account of Israel's history found in the Book of Exodus. Deuteronomy presents Moses reviewing that history for the assembled Israelites as they stand on the brink of their entry into the Promised Land. Similarly, 1 and 2 Chronicles review much of the history of Israel's monarchy from the reign of its first king, Saul, to the return from the Babylonian exile—materials also described in the books of 1 and 2 Samuel and 1 and 2 Kings. On a more subtle level, works such as the prophetic Book of Isaiah and the Psalms constantly draw on the earlier events of Israel's history and interpret their meaning for a later generation. Works such as Wisdom and Sirach reflect poetically on the creation accounts, casting them into meditations on the meaning of divine Wisdom.

The same is true of the New Testament, where there is an interrelationship among the various traditions (that is, the Christian community's memories about Jesus' teaching and ministry and the experiences of the earliest generation of Jesus' disciples) that would form the content of the New Testament. Also the connections made to the Old Testament within the writings of the New Testament are widespread and profound. Although there are many theories about this, there is no question that the three "synoptic Gospels" (so named because they can be "viewed in parallel") have a substantial interrelationship, with the most likely scenario being that both Matthew and Luke drew on Mark as a primary source for their own Gospel accounts of the life of Jesus.[2] Even Paul, whose letters contain minimal narrative material about the life of Jesus, still cites some key events that were part of the developing Gospel tradition.[3] Much more important, the New Testament writings draw

> The New Testament writings draw deeply on the Old Testament as an essential backdrop for their portrayal of Jesus and Christian identity and practice.

2   On this, see pages 72–84.

3   Paul is aware of Jesus' Davidic ancestry and his human birth (Romans 1:3), his Last Supper with his disciples (1 Corinthians 11:23); his Crucifixion and Resurrection appearances (1 Corinthians 15:1–8). 1 Timothy 6:13 refers to his execution under the reign of Pilate. There are, of course, numerous references to Jesus and his teaching, such as the love command (see 1 Corinthians 13) throughout Paul's writings.

deeply on the Old Testament as an essential backdrop for their por-trayal of Jesus and Christian identity and practice. In some cases this involves direct quotation of Old Testament writings, such as the so-called "formula quotations" of Matthew's Gospel that apply explicit Old Testament quotations to various aspects of Jesus' life and mis-sion.[4] In other cases, this dependence on the Old Testament is found in a multitude of allusions and types of characters or symbols found in the Old Testament. For example, in Jesus' silence before his accus-ers in Mark 14:61 we see an allusion to the silence of the suffering servant of Isaiah 53:7, and in the titles applied to Jesus that affirm his messianic identity we recognize the royal titles for the king of ancient Israel such as the "son of God" or "anointed one" (that is, the Messiah). On a broader scale, such profound Old Testament experi-ences as the account of creation, the exodus from Egypt, the leader-ship of Moses, the forging of the Sinai covenant, the role of the Temple and its priesthood, the experience of exile and a host of other Old Testament motifs are incorporated and reinterpreted within the various books and perspectives of the New Testament authors.[5]

Thus the Bible, for both Jews and Christians, is not a loose col-lection of diverse books, but an organic work of multiple parts, forged over time and woven together in complex and subtle ways.

The Makeup of the Old Testament

Whose Bible?

Affirming an inherent unity across the wide diversity of the biblical books does not mean that among those who claim the Bible as their Sacred Scriptures there is one agreed-upon number of biblical books and a uniform order of arrangement. Deciding the number of books to be included in the "Bible" and the order in which to place them was

---

4   See, for example, Matthew 1:22–23; 2:5–6, 15, and 17–18.

5   On this see Richard B. Hays, *Reading Backwards: Figural Christology and the Fourfold Gospel Witness* (Waco: Baylor University Press, 2014).

the result of a long process—for both Judaism and Christianity—that was not completed until long after the biblical books were written.

The Jewish Bible

Judaism includes twenty-four books within its Bible grouped into a threefold division, compressed into the acronym *"Tanak,"* derived from the first letter of the Hebrew words for each division, thus (1) the Pentateuch (*Torah*), (2) the Prophets (*Neviim*), and (3) the Writings (*Ketuvim*).

Table 1

The Jewish Bible—Tanak

The Five Books of Moses *Torah*	The Eight Books of the Prophets *Neviim*	The Eleven Books of the Writings *Ketuvim*
Genesis	**The "Former" Prophets**	Psalms
Exodus	Joshua	Proverbs
Leviticus	Judges	Job
Numbers	Samuel	Song of Songs
Deuteronomy	Kings	Ruth
		Lamentations
	The "Latter" Prophets	Ecclesiastes
	(which includes the	Esther
	twelve minor prophets	Daniel
	counted as one book)	Ezra/Nehemiah
	Isaiah	Chronicles
	Jeremiah	
	Ezekiel	
	The Twelve Minor Prophets	
	Hosea	
	Joel	
	Amos	
	Obadiah	
	Jonah	
	Micah	
	Nahum	
	Habakkuk	
	Zephaniah	
	Haggai	
	Zechariah	
	Malachi	

The Christian Bible

It is interesting to compare the list and sequence of the twenty-four books found in the Jewish canon with those of the forty-six books contained in the Christian Old Testament. While both groups have the same listing of the five books of the Pentateuch—the heart of the Old Testament Scriptures—significant differences appear in the rest of the Old Testament. Instead of a threefold overall division of the books as in the Jewish Bible, the Catholic version traditionally has a fourfold division.

Table 2

The Catholic Version of the Christian Bible

The Pentateuch	The Historical Books	The Wisdom Books	The Prophetic Books
(identical with the Jewish category of the Torah)	(which include some of what the Jewish Bible calls the "former prophets")	(which include the books found in the Jewish category of the "writings")	(which include several of the books found in the Jewish category of the "latter prophets," plus some books listed under the Jewish category of the "writings")
Genesis	Joshua	Job	Isaiah
Exodus	Judges	Psalms	Jeremiah
Leviticus	Ruth	Proverbs	Baruch (chapter
Numbers	1 Samuel	Ecclesiastes	6 = Epistle of
Deuteronomy	2 Samuel	Song of Songs	Jeremiah)
	1 Kings	Wisdom of	Ezekiel
	2 Kings	Solomon	Daniel
	1 Chronicles	Ecclesiasticus	Hosea
	2 Chronicles	(Sirach)	Joel
	Ezra		Amos
	Nehemiah		Obadiah
	Tobit		Jonah
	Judith		Micah
	Esther		Nahum
	1 Maccabees		Habakkuk
	2 Maccabees		Zephaniah
			Haggai
			Zechariah
			Malachi

How to explain these significant differences? Several factors are involved. One of the most important is that the Catholic order and number of Old Testament books draws heavily on the books contained in the Septuagint, the Greek version of the Old Testament mentioned earlier. When the Jewish sages eventually decided on which books to include in the Jewish canon, they based their choice on the Hebrew text, or what is called the Masoretic text, rather than on the Septuagint.[6] Thus some books that are included in the Catholic canon, such as Judith and Esther, 1 and 2 Maccabees, Tobit, Wisdom of Solomon, Baruch, and other books or segments thereof are not found in the Jewish Hebrew Bible.

Other reasons for the differences between the number of books included in the Septuagint but not absorbed into the Hebrew (that is, Masoretic) text include the probability that in the first couple of centuries when both the early Christian community and the Jewish community were in the process of determining which books belonged in their respective Bibles, some books used by Christians to apply to Christ were thereby excluded from the Jewish canon. Jews reverenced these books as sacred but not inspired.

In addition, distinctive theological visions may underlie the different order of the books in Judaism and Christianity. The Jewish canon tracks the origin and development of the people Israel, which appears to reach its summit with the monarchy under David and then his son and successor Solomon. A long period of decline and suffering follows that summit, climaxing in the Babylonian exile. This tragic history ends, however, on a hopeful note. At the conclusion of 2 Chronicles, the final book of the Jewish Bible, the Persian emperor Cyrus, considered by the Bible as an instrument of God's providence, decrees that the Jews may return to their homeland. By contrast, the sequence of the Christian Old Testament order ends with the challenging but hopeful prophecy of Malachi, a biblical

---

6   The Hebrew term *masorah*, meaning tradition, or that which is set or fettered, is quoted in Ezekiel 20:37 and came to be applied to a quasi-official version of the Hebrew Bible endorsed by rabbinic Judaism.

vision seen by Christians as opening the way to the advent of Jesus the Messiah.

Different Christian Bibles

We should note that there are also differences among the Catholic, Protestant, and Orthodox listing of Old Testament books. Here again, both the use of the Septuagint and tension between various Christian traditions played a role in determining those differences. Although the list of Old Testament books had remained mostly uniform through the early centuries of the Church, at the time of the Reformation, Protestant leaders chose to revert to the listing of Old Testament books found in the Hebrew or Masoretic text rather than the Septuagint listing. For example, Martin Luther, in his 1534 translation of the Bible, excluded several books that he considered "apocryphal" (from the Greek word "hidden"; understood to mean "doubtful authenticity") and had them printed in the back of the Bible—namely, 1 Esdras, 2 Esdras, Tobit, Judith, Wisdom of Solomon, Ecclesiasticus, Baruch, the Letter of Jeremiah, Prayer of Manasseh, and 1 and 2 Maccabees. He judged that these were venerable and useful books, but were not inspired. Roman Catholics, however, continued to include these works as inspired parts of the Bible. Catholics refer to them as "deuterocanonical" ("deutero" is from the Greek word for "second," so the term implicitly recognizes that these inspired books play a less prominent role in the Bible); that is, inspired books that were not part of the Hebrew Bible yet remain as valid parts of Sacred Scripture.

There are also some minor differences between the list of Old Testament books found in Roman Catholicism and Orthodox Christianity. But, more importantly, both Christian traditions accept the sequence and listing of books drawn from the Septuagint.

These differences, which were once matters of bitter dispute, have tempered over time, particularly as ecumenical relations among Catholics, Protestants, and Orthodox Christians have vastly improved. All Christians consider the so-called apocryphal books as sacred and useful, if not inspired, and many Protestant editions of the Bible include these books in a special section of the Bible between the Old and the New Testament.

The Makeup of the New Testament

When we turn to the New Testament things are much simpler! All Christians—Catholic, Protestant, and Orthodox—generally agree on the list and order of the New Testament books. As already noted, the overall sequence of books has a quasi-chronological order, with the four Gospel accounts of Matthew, Mark, Luke, and John coming first, since they concern the life, mission, Death, and Resurrection of Jesus. Then follows the Acts of the Apostles, which traces the evolution of the early community from its origin in Jerusalem, out into the Mediterranean world, concluding with Paul arriving in Rome under house arrest. The Pauline letters come next, even though from the point of view of literary sequence, the letters of Paul were written before the Gospels. These are followed by the rest of the New Testament writings, without any particular connection with the chronology of the early Church itself. The Book of Revelation appropriately ends the New Testament canon with its vision of the New Jerusalem and the Risen Christ triumphing over the demonic powers.

Hebrew Scriptures or Old Testament?

There is one final issue we should consider when exploring the nature of the Bible. This question arises from the newfound respect for the Jewish roots of Christianity that thankfully has characterized the recent decades of the Church. How should Christians refer to what we traditionally call the "Old Testament"? For some this terminology appears to disparage the Jewish Scriptures. "Old" implies that the religion and traditions of Judaism are obsolete; now surpassed and superseded by Christianity and its "New" Testament. In fact, that perspective appears to be affirmed in the Letter to the Hebrews (9:15) when it declares that Christ is the mediator of a "new covenant" that surpasses the former covenant. The Greek word used here for "covenant" is *diatheke*, which means a formal agreement or a "testament."

In the light of this concern, some scholars prefer to refer to the Old Testament as the "Hebrew Scriptures" or the "First Testament." However, such terms bring their own problems. While the designation "Hebrew Scriptures" is fully appropriate for Jews, it is not accurate from a Christian point of view. Christians should fully respect the integrity and propriety of the Hebrew Scriptures for Jews.[7] These are their Sacred Scriptures, emerging from the history and faith of Judaism, and are essential for their religious self-understanding. Christians, on the other hand, have gratefully appropriated the writings of the Hebrew Scriptures, but now view them from the vantage point of *Christian faith*. A Christian reading of the Old Testament is different because of this central reality of faith in Jesus Christ as the fulfillment of the hopes expressed in the Scriptures and in the history of God's people. Therefore, the Old Testament is no longer for Christians simply the "Hebrew" Scriptures but an essential part of the Christian Scriptures.

"Old" when applied to the Old Testament means "venerable," "fundamental," and "first" within the sequence of sacred history.

The terms "old" and "new" need not be read as if they meant respectively "obsolete" and "up-to-date." In many cultures, particularly more traditional ones, someone or something that is "old" is most worthy of respect. Similarly, "old" when applied to the Old Testament means "venerable," "fundamental," and "first" within the sequence of sacred history. Likewise, "new" does not have to be understood as implying that the "old" is to be discarded and replaced. The New Testament is "new" in the sense that it represents, from the viewpoint of Christian faith, the

---

7   "Christians can and ought to admit that the Jewish reading of the Bible is a possible one, in continuity with the Jewish Sacred Scriptures from the Second Temple period, a reading analogous to the Christian reading which developed in parallel fashion" (The Pontifical Biblical Commission, *The Jewish People and Their Sacred Scriptures in the Christian Bible* [Libreria Editrice Vaticana, 2002], 22).

unfolding of God's plan of salvation that has now come to its climax with the advent of Christ. For the earliest Christians, their Bible was the Old Testament. When Paul, for example, appeals to the "scriptures" (see 1 Corinthians 15:3–4), he means what we call the Old Testament. The early Christians would never dream of considering the Scriptures of Israel as "obsolete," but rather saw the Scriptures as the essential backdrop and normative guide for understanding the mission of Jesus Christ. Seen in this manner, the traditional designations, Old and New Testaments, should be preferred.

Conclusion: The Rich Diversity of the One Bible

This review of the components of the Bible reminds us how rich and complex this "book" is. Part of that diversity comes from the many literary forms that make up the Bible, as well as the unfolding cultural backdrop of Israel and the early Church that left its imprint on the biblical writers and the events they portray. The diversity and complexity of the Bible also stem from the different, if closely related, religious traditions at play. Judaism and Christianity are, of course, substantially different, while at the same time the New Testament books affirm the vital connection between them. Different religious perspectives also characterize Christianity and, in the case of determining the number of Old Testament books, for example, the theological and ecclesiastical differences between Catholics and Protestants—particularly in the heat of the Reformation—were decisive.

CHAPTER 2

The History of the Bible: The Emergence of the Old Testament

This chapter focuses on how the Old Testament writings themselves emerged within the unfolding span of Israel's history. As noted earlier, we should not assume that individual books of the Old Testament were produced in conjunction with the period of history they portray. Some books describing the earliest periods of Israel's story were composed in written form much later.

Tracking the History of Israel

Becoming aware of the periods of Israel's history as presented in the Bible and linking that history with corresponding biblical books can help give us a fuller picture of the Old Testament landscape.

1. Prehistory

The opening chapters (1–12) of Genesis, the first book of the Bible, deal with what we might call Israel's "prehistory," describing the creation of the universe and the origins of the human family. These early stories are obviously not intended as "historical" accounts in the way we view history today. These epic stories—God's creation of the world and of the human family, the tragedy of the sins of Adam and Eve, the violence of Cain and Abel, the flood and God's covenant with Noah, or the Tower of Babel—are not frivolous or without significance. They affirm fundamental biblical convictions about the nature of God as Creator and Redeemer, about the capacity of the human person, male and female, to relate to God (since they have been made in the divine image, Genesis 1:26), about the origin and ongoing realty of evil in the world, and about God's enduring and providential presence within history. These stories are "myths" in the strictest sense of that term—not simple fiction, but narrative accounts of the Bible's deepest convictions about God, about creation as a gift of God, and about the origin of the human family and its destiny.

With the stories of the patriarchs and matriarchs, Genesis (chapters 12–50) turns to the remote origins of the people Israel. The historical time period that parallels this section of Genesis is approximately 1900 to 1300 BC. Abraham is summoned by God to set out with his clan from his ancestral home of Ur (present-day Iraq) for the land that later will be the "Promised Land." Abraham and Sarah are seen as the "parents" of God's people, and Abraham's faith, displayed in his willingness to sacrifice Isaac in obedience to God (Genesis 22), seals his exemplary role. From the stories of Abraham and his descendants, including the sojourn in Egypt in the period from Joseph to Moses, will flow the preparation for the exodus, the Sinai Covenant, and the ultimate possession of the land.

2. The Exodus

The books of Exodus, Leviticus, Numbers, and Deuteronomy complete the Pentateuch and cover a crucial period in the biblical saga, namely the subjugation of the Jews in Egypt; their miraculous rescue by God under the leadership of Moses; their long desert sojourn where their fidelity to God is sorely tested, yet also where God forges the Sinai Covenant, making them "God's People"; and finally, through God's providence, their arrival at the border of the Promised Land. These biblical books are not simply chronicling historical events that shaped the people of Israel, but are shot through with the Bible's fundamental theology. They proclaim God's fidelity to his people; they present the demands of God's will expressed in the covenant values, practices, and rituals that constituted true obedience to God; and they call for humility and repentance in response to God's graciousness and the people's recurring failures. The parallel historical period covered by this part of the biblical story is roughly from 1300 to 1250 BC. The Bible retells the story of Israel's advance from Egypt to the Promised Land as a dramatic single, if extended, event. Historians affirm that this is a simplification of the actual unfolding of events and the precise dating of this period is sharply debated. It is likely that the migration of Hebrew tribes into the land of Canaan took place in piecemeal fashion, with some merger of migrant tribes with the local peoples who already inhabited the highlands area of what would later become the land of Israel.

The Sources of the Pentateuch

While later biblical tradition assumed that Moses was the author of the Pentateuch (see, for example, Ezra 3:2, which refers to the Pentateuch as the "law of Moses"), modern biblical scholarship has detected various streams of traditions, (that is, the various stories and perspectives handed on through successive generations) that fused together in the composition of these biblical books. The different names assigned to God in Genesis—that is, *Elohim* in Genesis 1 and *Yahweh elohim* in Genesis 2 and 3—led scholars, already in the seventeenth century, to suggest that there were at least two different sources present here; one that would be designated as the "Elohist" and the other as the "Yahwist." But as literary analysis of the Bible advanced, later scholars would suggest that *four* different strands of tradition were to be found in the Pentateuch: (1) the "Priestly" source, responsible, for example, for the elegant and hymn-like story of creation in Genesis 1 and 2; (2) the "Yahwist" account, that dominates the narrative structure of the Pentateuch and that tended to present God in anthropomorphic ways (for example, walking and talking with Adam and Eve in the Garden of Eden or engaging face to face with Moses at Sinai); (3) the "Elohist" source that included a number of stories from Israel's early history (such as the accounts of Jacob and his clan and the rise of Moses as the leader of the Israelites); and (4) the Deuteronomist source that accounts for the unique literary and theological characteristics of the Book of Deuteronomy and its perspective on Israel's early history.

Modern biblical scholars still debate what sources formed the Pentateuch and in what stages it was composed. As we will note, the final written form of the Pentateuch would not appear until after the period of the exile in the sixth century BC, yet it is also true that the origin of many of the narratives and traditions incorporated in the first five books of the Bible reach back into the formative period of Israel's history.

3. The Possession of the Land and the Early Period in Israel

This period is covered mainly by the books of Joshua and Judges and by the early chapters of 1 Samuel. The events take place roughly from the conclusion of the exodus (about 1250 BC) to the period of the establishment of the monarchy, when Saul emerged as king in approximately 1020 BC. The Book of Joshua describes the dramatic conquest of Canaan under the successor of Moses after the crossing of the Jordan River at Jericho. Although the Bible sees this as an unstoppable process on the part of the Israelite armies, archaeology and even some hints in the Bible itself suggest that this was a long period—some of it involving military action and some the result of the gradual social, economic, and political dominance of the Hebrew tribes over the local populations in the Judean highlands.

The Book of Judges and the early part of 1 Samuel cover the initial social organization of the various Hebrew tribes under the period of the "judges" who were, in fact, the leaders of the various clans or tribes that made up the Hebrew people. This loose federation of tribes would gradually evolve into the united monarchy under David and Solomon. From the point of view of the Bible, this evolving social and political situation in the central highlands of what later was named Judah was a sign of God's fidelity to his promises to his people. The struggle with the Canaanites who already inhabited the region was similarly viewed as a victory of God's people over the pagan tribes. Issues of Israel's fidelity to the covenant and trust in God's providential care continue to be an integral part of the biblical story.

4. The Monarchy

This part of the biblical history covers a long period that witnesses the rise of the monarchy, its highpoint under David and Solomon, and its long travails as a divided kingdom under their successors—leading up to the loss of the Northern Kingdom of Israel under the Assyrians and the tragedy of the Babylonian exile that later befalls the Southern Kingdom of Judah. This period is accounted for in the books of 1 and 2 Samuel and 1 and 2 Kings, as well as the more or less parallel account in 1 and 2 Chronicles. The first anointed king was Saul, who was a charismatic judge but an erratic monarch. Saul's demise leads to the emergence of David, who would remain in the eye of the Bible as a unique and compelling figure despite his evident flaws. The reign of David (around 1010 to 970 BC) united the northern and southern tribes, extended the boundaries of Israel, and eventually brought the capital to Jerusalem, which David established as both the political and religious center of his united kingdom. His son Solomon (970–931 BC) consolidated David's gains and replaced the simple sanctuary David had begun in Jerusalem with the first constructed Temple—thus introducing a major innovation in the religious life of the biblical peoples, one whose influence and symbolism endured down through the New Testament period itself, even after its eventual destruction by the Romans in AD 70.

With rare exceptions, the lineup of kings who follow David and Solomon are, certainly from the Bible's point of view, grand disappointments: they lacked backbone and failed to trust in God's providence in the face of threat, failed to protect the poor and vulnerable, and succumbed to the seduction of the vices and false gods of the surrounding cultures. Trouble begins almost immediately after the death of Solomon, when under his son and successor Rehoboam (reigned 932–915 BC) the seam between the northern and southern tribes splits and the once-united kingdom of Israel is divided into Israel in the north and Judah in the south (around 932 or 931). The northern kingdom would be dissolved under the impact of the Assyrian invasion (722 or 721 BC), with its leading classes led into exile and other peoples brought in to populate the northern region; an early example of "ethnic cleansing." The southern kingdom of Judah would survive for a little longer, but had to live under submission to Assyria's dominance of the region. Ultimately the Babylonian Empire of Nebuchadnezzar supplanted Assyria, and the Kingdom of Judah then suffered a fate comparable to that of the north, with two devastating invasions (598 BC and 587 BC) and a calamitous exile (586 to 539 BC). The exile signaled the apparent end of the monarchy and the destruction of Jerusalem and its Temple. The deportation of most of the leading classes of Judah was also tantamount to losing the land—a triple blow to Israel's identity and its hope.

The Prophetic Movement

Another phenomenon of this period was the rise of the prophetic movement in Israel. Ironically, at the moment in history when the monarchy would lead Israel to its widest expansion and greatest internal prosperity, its traditional ideals would begin to erode and crumble. The origins of the prophetic movement began with bands of charismatic prophets who challenged Israel's establishment and accused it of departing from its original ideals forged in its desert sojourn and its pioneering beginnings in the Promised Land. Two of the most important figures from this early

> The exile signaled the apparent end of the monarchy, the destruction of Jerusalem and its Temple, and the deportation of Judah's leading classes.

period (early ninth century BC) were the prophet Elijah and his disciple Elisha. Elijah railed against the excesses of the northern monarchy, particularly under the reign of King Ahab and his infamous pagan consort, Jezebel. The exploits of Elijah and Elisha (both of whom are cited in the Gospels as antecedents to Jesus' prophetic ministry; see, for example, Luke 4:25–27) are recounted in 1 and 2 Kings. Following upon these iconic prophets comes a series of prophets whose oracles and sharp challenges to the kings and ruling class of Judah become the "conscience of Israel," figures such as the "writing" prophets Isaiah, Jeremiah, Amos, and Hosea. Their declarations, retained and edited by their disciples, also held up the highest ideals of ancient Israel, drawing on motifs and values from Israel's past to inspire reform and the creation of a new and faithful Israelite community.

5. Exile and Return

There is little direct historical narrative about the life of the Judean exiles in Babylon, apart from the kind of popular stories found in biblical books such as Esther, Judith, and Tobit. Psalm 137 captures the suffering and poignancy of this period in biblical history:

> By the rivers of Babylon
>   there we sat weeping
>   when we remembered Zion.
> On the poplars in its midst
>   we hung up our harps.
> For there our captors asked us
>   for the words of a song;
> Our tormentors, for joy:
>   "Sing for us a song of Zion!"
> But how could we sing a song of the LORD
>   in a foreign land? (Psalm 137:1–4).

This period left a profound impression upon the biblical consciousness, and following this period many biblical books were composed, including the latter parts of Isaiah, the books of Jeremiah, Ezekiel, parts of the Psalms, Jonah, the visions of the Book of Daniel, and the prophetic hopes of Joel and Malachi, to name a few. During this period, too, other major sections of the Bible were solidified in writing, including the Pentateuch itself.

The exile ended with the triumph of Persia over Babylon. As noted in Second Chronicles, Cyrus the Great issued a decree (538 BC) allowing peoples who had been subjugated under the Babylonians to return to their native place and to rebuild, and this included the Jews, who could now return to Jerusalem and Judea. This begins the postexilic period within the history of the Bible. The returning exiles would begin to rebuild Jerusalem and its sanctuary, the region of Judah now being a small and modest enclave, still within the orbit of Persian influence. From the Bible's point of view, this would be a time of revival of hope, a return to the sources of their faith expressed in the Mosaic Law, and a renewed trust in God's care for Israel. These modest beginnings are noted in the biblical books of Ezra and Nehemiah and this period of reform set the foundation for the character of Jewish life that led up to the time of Jesus and the New Testament.

Hellenistic Influence

As already noted in chapter 1, a significant turn of events in this postexilic period began with the invasion of Alexander the Great, whose armies came to the region in 329 BC. With Alexander (who died shortly after in 323 BC), there was a strong influx of Hellenistic culture into Jewish life, affecting especially the ruling classes. The political and economic life of Israel was dominated by the Greek dynasties set up in the wake of Alexander's death with first the Ptolemaic dynasty ruling from Egypt (323–198 BC), and then under the rival and more oppressive rule of the Seleucids (198 to about 140 BC). As narrated in 1 and 2 Maccabees, armed resistance to the rule of the Seleucids ruling from Damascus ushered in a century of Jewish rule (about 140 to 63 BC), restoring the ancient hopes associated with the Davidic dynasty and once more uniting and expanding the borders of Israel to include the areas that had been the northern and southern kingdoms under David and Solomon. But this interlude of freedom was doomed to failure, as the Hasmonean dynasty became increasingly corrupt and inept, casting itself as a priestly dynasty and assimilating Greek culture. The failures of the Hasmonean dynasty triggered a series of reactions and divisions within Judaism, leading ultimately to reform movements such as that of the Pharisees who aspired to renew Israel by making fidelity to the Law and religious purity accessible to ordinary Jews. Another type of reaction was that of the Essenes, a sectarian reform movement that preferred to withdraw in protest at the excesses of Hasmonean Jerusalem and await God's final purifying judgment. The sectarian group that lived in the Judean desert at Qumran and preserved a library of both biblical and sectarian documents (the Dead Sea Scrolls) was undoubtedly part of the Essene movement.

The divisions and civil strife that inundated Judaism during this period led ultimately to civil war. In 63 BC Jews invited the Romans under the Emperor Pompey, whose empire was now extended into the Eastern Mediterranean region, to arbitrate. The Romans came and never left until nearly eight centuries later. In the civil war between Antipater, the father of Herod the Great, and other Jewish factions (approximately 63 to 37 BC), the Romans sided with the Herodians and later installed Herod the Great as vassal king over the region formerly ruled by the Hasmoneans. And thus the historical period embraced by the Old Testament came to an end, with the social and religious context in place that came to be the world in which Jesus and the early Christian community lived.

6. An Alternate Track: The Wisdom Literature

There is another stream of tradition in the Old Testament, very different in style and perspective from the Pentateuch or the prophetic and historical books we have been considering. The so-called "wisdom literature" is very similar to other such traditions in the Middle East that drew upon proverbial human experience, the circumstances of family life, and the beauty of nature to reflect upon what defines a virtuous life and human destiny. This style of reflection goes far back into Middle Eastern history. The wisdom books in the Bible do not often refer to God's intervention in history and, in fact, give little attention to the history of Israel as God's people—the subject of the other books of the Bible. This focus on human experience and creation itself gives the wisdom literature a more universal scope. Such books as Proverbs, Job, Ecclesiastes (also known by its Hebrew name of Qoheleth), Ecclesiasticus (its Hebrew name is Sirach), and the Wisdom of Solomon are considered "wisdom literature." Some of the psalms might also fit in this category such as Psalm 1, 19, 37, 49, 73, 111, and 119. Some also consider the Song of Songs to be part of Israel's wisdom literature. Although its style is very different from the proverbial reflections of other wisdom books, it has a "secular" tone and draws its poetry from the human experience of love. Poetic reflections in books such as Proverbs, Sirach, and the Wisdom of Solomon use the metaphor of "wisdom" as a kind of personification of God's presence within the very structure of creation and the movements of human history (see, for example, Proverbs 8). This dimension of the wisdom literature influenced some of the New Testament authors in their reflection on the mystery of Jesus' identity, such as in the prologue to John's Gospel.[1]

> This focus on human experience and creation itself gives the wisdom literature a more universal scope.

The Emergence of the Old Testament Scriptures

As we have seen, the horizon of the Old Testament covers a wide swath of history, beginning with the remote origins of the human family in the creation accounts of Genesis, and then moving from

---

1 For example, John's references to the Word as the pattern of creation (John 1:3) and the Word's dwelling among humans (literally, "setting up his tent") echo the reflection on divine Wisdom in Proverbs 8:22–31 and Sirach 24:1–8.

the forging of the people Israel in the events of the Exodus and the Sinai Covenant down to the modest restoration of Judah in the post-exilic period. Tracing the appearance of the Old Testament Scriptures themselves within that span of history is a complex and challenging question. Again, without getting bogged down in a myriad of details and scholarly debates, we can try to get a general sense of how the Old Testament books emerged against the backdrop of Israel's unfolding history.

Oral Tradition

At the outset, we need to appreciate the significant role of oral tradition in the development and maintenance of the content that eventually becomes part of the written books of the Bible.[2] Our modern culture—particularly in developed countries—depends to an enormous degree on written and, now, digital materials. Thus it is difficult for us to understand the dynamics and the reliability of oral transmission. For much of human history down to the modern period, relatively few people could read or write. Written materials did exist in the ancient world, such as hieroglyphics in Egypt, whose forms appear as early as 4000 BC. The remote origins of cuneiform writing in Mesopotamia also began around this time and became a standard alphabet around 1000 BC. Thousands of clay tables containing court records and other written materials have been found dating back to this period in various parts of the Middle East. Yet writing (and reading) was mainly the preserve of professional "scribes," or a few educated elites who were literate and had the skills necessary for the task of maintaining written materials.

Oral transmission of information and traditions remained the normal mode of communication. Unlike a written tablet or parchment, oral transmission was not a thing but an "event" that required a speaker and a listener or, more likely, several listeners. What was

---

2   On this subject, see the very helpful study of Eric Eve, *Behind the Gospels: Understanding the Oral Tradition* (Minneapolis: Fortress, 2014). Although his focus is on the Gospels, his analysis of oral tradition in general is valuable.

being communicated was not "seen" but "heard"—thus an essential part of oral transmission is its reception by an audience, and the content of the oral transmission could be fortified by such things as tone of voice, gestures, and facial expressions. Oral transmission usually took place in a specific social context such as a group of people gathered to pray or to celebrate some significant occasion. These circumstances, too, were part of the communication process and left their imprint on how tradition was shaped.

> Unlike a written tablet or parchment, oral transmission was not a thing but an "event."

To facilitate memory, much ancient literature was shaped in a particular way, such as using poetry with a set cadence and repetition of thoughts, linking segments of information with similar words, and preferring relative brevity or economy of words. There could also be a connection between some written notes and oral transmission. Oral commentary could expand on such notes and use the written materials as an aid for memory and oral communication. Even after materials were committed to writing, oral tradition did not necessarily stop, but continued to be an important means of communication.

Such a speaking and listening mode of communication is far less developed for modern peoples who can depend on the written word. With less and less need or opportunity for moderns to use their memories, particularly in communicating literature or vital information, that capacity diminishes. Yet the ancient world was acutely dependent on memory, and still today some traditional societies depend on oral transmission. Many devout Muslims, for example, are able to recite the entire Koran by heart.

The Written Books of the Bible

Thus in turning to the formation of the Bible, we have to keep in mind that many of the traditions that worked their way into the Bible were first formulated and communicated orally, and in some circumstances used a mixture of oral and written documentation. Against that back-drop we can find within the Bible itself some reference to the emergence of the written form of the biblical materials. Often this is linked with liturgical celebrations or gatherings for worship and instruction.

Deuteronomy, which presents itself as a review of the key events of the Exodus, is one of the first biblical books to refer to its written form. In Deuteronomy 17:18–19 Moses counsels the people about any future king of Israel they may set over them after they have entered the Promised Land: "He shall write a copy of this law upon a scroll from the one that is in the custody of the levitical priests. It shall remain with him and he shall read it as long as he lives, so that he may learn to fear the Lord, his God, and to observe carefully all the words of this law and these statutes" (see also references to Deuteronomy as the law "written in this book" in 28:58; 29:19; and the instruction to "read this law aloud" to the people in 31:11). Although rhetorically it places itself in the days of Moses, Deuteronomy was not composed until the reform movement of King Josiah in the seventh century BC and was probably subject to further revisions until it reached its final written form in the postexilic period around 500 BC.

Tradition credits Moses as being the author of the entire Pentateuch. Exodus 24 portrays Moses communicating with God on Mount Sinai and then writing down what God had told him. This act of writing God's words, as the passage describes it, takes place in the context of a liturgical celebration. Moses descended from the mountain top and "wrote down all the words of the Lord and, rising early the morning, he built at the foot of the mountain an altar and twelve sacred stones for the twelve tribes of Israel" (Exodus 24:4). There then follows a sacrifice of young bulls, and the sprinkling of the altar and the people with the blood of the bulls to seal the moment. Yet, as already noted, it is highly improbable that Moses was the literary author of these first five books of the Bible, even as the Bible affirms he was the source of these sacred traditions.

The reform introduced by Josiah (641–610 BC) was a significant moment in the development of the Bible. It was during his reign that the Second Book of Kings recounts the dramatic discovery by the high priest Hilkiah of the written book of the Law of Moses in the Temple. The account suggests that apparently it had languished there during a long period of neglect in the religious life of Israel. The high priest gives the book to the scribe Shaphan (who, as a scribe, is able to read). When the contents of the book are read to the king, he is seized with remorse. He summons "all the elders of Judah and of Jerusalem" and has the entire "book of the covenant" (2 Kings 23:1–2) read to them. While the reform movement of Josiah no doubt revived the role of the Law of Moses in the life of Israel, it is unlikely that the full-blown written Pentateuch was in existence at this time.

The most important milestone in the written production of the Old Testament (as distinct from older traditions handed down through oral tradition) takes place after the exile when, under the leadership of Ezra and Nehemiah, the people of Judah rebuild their Temple and their Jewish way of life. No doubt the experience of the exile was a trigger for a deeper reflection on the part of the people concerning their religious heritage. Nevertheless, when Ezra reads the Law of Moses before the assembled people, it seems to be a new discovery for all concerned (read the striking description of this dramatic event in Nehemiah 8:1–12), similar to the discovery of the neglected book of the Law during the reign of King Josiah. During this postexilic period there would be an explosion of written materials appearing, including the Pentateuch itself, the historical and prophetic books, and much of the Book of Psalms and wisdom literature. Writing later in this same postexilic period, Jesus ben Sira, the author of Ecclesiasticus, praises by name the authors of several individual biblical books (see Ben Sira,

During this postexilic period there would be an explosion of written materials appearing, including the Pentateuch itself.

sometimes called Sirach 49). The author of 2 Maccabees notes that Nehemiah had collected "books about the kings and the prophets, and the books of David, and the royal letters about votive offerings" (2 Maccabees 2:13). Judas Maccabeus is also praised because he "collected for us all the books that had been scattered because of the war, and we now have them in our possession. If you need them, send messengers to get them for you" (2 Maccabees 2:14–15).

Several Jewish texts from the later postexilic period testify to collections of the biblical writings, such as two from the second century AD: 4 Ezra and the rabbinic text Baba Batra—each of which refers to twenty-four biblical books grouped in the three traditional divisions of the Law, the Prophets, and the Writings. And we know from the discoveries of the Dead Sea Scrolls at Qumran, the Jewish sect that settled there from the middle of the second century BC had written copies of every book of the Bible except that of Esther (a book whose inclusion in the Jewish canon would be sharply debated because it does not mention God).

Conclusion: History Handed On in Diverse Forms and with Different Interpretations

The traditions about the history of Israel stretching from the stories of the exodus down through the monarchy and the periods of exile and return were handed on within the community of Israel in a variety of settings: they were recounted to the assembly at worship, at great moments of celebration, or at critical moments of reform. No doubt the institutions of the monarchy and the priesthood, both intimately related, played a key role in the maintenance of this tradition and its eventual solidification in written form. This rich and varied tradition was never meant to simply be the collective memory of past historical events. Reviewing and reinterpreting that history was a fundamentally religious process, reminding Israel of its covenant with God and of the responsibilities that flowed from that covenant.

Deciding which of these books should be included in the Jewish canon—that is, revered as not only sacred but inspired—would not be determined until beyond the first century AD. That will be a subject of a later chapter.

CHAPTER 3

The History of the New Testament: From Jesus to the Post-Resurrection Community

In the last chapter, we saw that the Old Testament had a long period of development before its various books took shape in writing. We now turn to a similar but much briefer period that led to the formation of the New Testament writings.

The Span of New Testament History

The historical period in which the New Testament appeared is far less extensive than that of the Old Testament. The Gospel accounts of Matthew and Luke place Jesus' birth under the rule of King Herod the Great, who died around 4 BC. The close of the New Testament period is around the end of the first century. Thus the more than two thousand years of history covered in the Old Testament far outstrips the one hundred years of the New Testament's horizon. Despite the shorter time span, deciphering the historical evolution of the New Testament also has its challenges.

While the Gospel accounts and Acts give us something of a chronological sequence, moving from the life, Death, and Resurrection of Jesus to the subsequent life of the early Church, the rest of the New Testament books provide few hints about the precise chronology of the early Church. Likewise, as we will see, the actual writing of the four Gospel accounts, the Acts of the Apostles, the letters of Paul, and the other New Testament texts does not correspond with the historical sequence of the events they describe.

Roman Palestine at the Time of Jesus

Jesus of Nazareth was born and died during a turbulent period in the history of the Jewish people. Some sixty years before Jesus' birth, Rome entered into the arena of Israel, marking the end of a century of Jewish independence under the Hasmonean dynasty. At first Rome entrusted the rule of the region to Herod the Great (40–4 BC), a dominant and clever figure who was known for his cruelty (especially to his own family), for his shrewd way of dealing with his Roman patrons, and for his remarkable capacity to build great cities and monuments.[1] Among his building projects was the substantial expansion and renewal of the Jerusalem Temple, which was one of the largest human structures in the world at the time of its completion.

When Herod died, the Romans divided his kingdom into three smaller entities or "ethnarchies" and appointed Herod's three sons as rulers: Herod Philip ruled in the north and eastern part of the country, what was known as Upper Galilee because it is a mountainous region; another son, Herod Antipas, ruled Lower Galilee that stretched from the Sea of Galilee west to the Mediterranean coast. The third son, Archelaus, was given the region of Judea and Samaria, the important southern section of "Palestine," as it was called by the Romans.[2] Archelaus proved to be inept and vicious, so much so that the Romans removed him from power in AD 6, banishing him to Gaul. From that time on the Romans exercised direct rule over these key provinces of Judea and Samaria. In its narrative about the birth and infancy of Jesus, Matthew's Gospel confirms Archelaus' reputation for cruelty. After the Holy Family's sojourn in Egypt (fleeing from the murderous intent of Herod the Great, the father of Archelaus), Joseph fears to go back to his home region of Judea and decides to take his

---

1   See Adam Koman Marshak, *The Many Faces of Herod the Great* (Grand Rapids: Eerdmans, 2015).

2   The Romans deliberately named the region "Palestine," referring to the Philistines, the ancient enemies of the Jews. Using the term "Roman Palestine" for this area intends no political implications for the modern conflict between the State of Israel and the Palestinians.

wife and son north to the town of Nazareth in the region of Galilee (Matthew 2:22).

The Mission of Jesus in the Context of Roman Palestine

These political events set the stage for Jesus' own life. When he is warned by some friendly Pharisees that Herod Antipas was seeking to kill him, Jesus calls the ruler a "fox" and defiantly states that his mission would continue despite the threat (see Luke 13:31–33). Jesus eventually left the Galilean region where Antipas ruled and went south to Judea and its capital Jerusalem. Since Jesus was arrested in Jerusalem, he thereby fell under Roman jurisdiction and thus became liable to crucifixion, the notorious Roman form of capital punishment. Reflecting the political nuances of the time, Luke once again ushers Herod Antipas onto the stage at the time of Jesus' trial before Pilate, when, as a courtesy, Pilate sends his prisoner to Herod Antipas when he learns that Jesus is a Galilean. But Herod treats Jesus as a fool and sends him back to Pilate (see Luke 23:6–11).

The Gospel accounts tell the story of Jesus from the vantage point of faith in his Resurrection.[3] They are not meant to be dispassionate reviews of the historical circumstances of Jesus' life and times. They are faith-filled proclamations of "good news"—testifying that the one who announced the coming reign of God and who healed and taught with grace and authority was in fact God's Messiah, and even more, the embodiment of God's loving presence in the world. The Gospel accounts were directed to believers in order to strengthen their faith in Christ and to instruct and inspire them to live in accord with the teaching and example of Jesus.

Yet the Gospels describe the vibrant mission of Jesus in a way that reliably reflects the actual historical circumstances of early first-century Roman Palestine. As we will note later, John's Gospel is very

---

3   See chapter 4 , pages 44–59.

different in its portrayal of Jesus' life and in the literary form in which it presents the teaching of Jesus. Yet this Gospel account is well aware of the topography of Jerusalem at the time of Jesus and is also familiar with the contours of the Galilee region. In all four Gospel accounts the life of Jesus plays out in an arena that is stretched between the twin poles of Galilee in the north and Jerusalem, the center of Judea, in the south. Jerusalem and its Temple formed the religious heart of Jewish life. Jewish pilgrims (including Jesus and his family) would travel to Jerusalem for the great feasts of Passover, Pentecost, and Succoth (also called the Feast of Tabernacles or Booths). The priests and ruling elites were under the jurisdiction of Rome, but were still entrusted with keeping order in the capital, particularly at volatile times such as the Passover, when the population of the area would swell to possibly three times its normal size. The Roman procurators, who were the Emperor's on-site delegates, ruled from Caesarea Maritima on the Mediterranean coast, a harbor city that had been built by Herod the Great. They would come up to Jerusalem to make their presence felt, particularly at times of tension, such as during the pilgrim feasts. A significant Roman garrison was billeted in the Antonianum Fortress that was built into the northwest corner of the Temple enclosure.

> Jerusalem and its Temple formed the religious heart of Jewish life.

The region of Galilee where Jesus grew up and where most of his disciples were recruited was an agrarian society, with many small farming villages and a few larger towns. The difficult economic circumstances we read about in the Gospels accurately reflect conditions in the region at this time. Most of the population were peasant farmers, eking out a subsistence living, often working land that was owned by absentee landowners to whom they would owe tribute in the form of a significant portion of the crops the farmers raised. Other taxation, often in the form of tolls, was levied by the ruling authorities as the peasants brought their goods to market. The Sea of

Galilee, with its rich stock of fish, was another economic resource for those who lived in its vicinity. Smoked fish from this body of fresh water was exported to other parts of the Roman Empire. So, too, was garum, a kind of fermented fish paste favored by Roman cuisine. The Gospels attest that several of Jesus' disciples were recruited from families who owned boats and were Galilean fishermen.

In contrast to Jerusalem, and apart from the city of Caesarea Maritima, relatively few Roman troops were stationed in the Galilee region. But substantial numbers of Roman troops were stationed in Syria, just over the Golan Heights and only a few days' march from the region of Galilee. Other soldiers who served the Herodian rulers would see to civil order on an ordinary basis. Matthew and Luke's Gospels refer to a centurion who lived near Capernaum, a border town between the regions ruled by Herod Antipas and Herod Phillip (see Matthew 8:5–13 and Luke 7:1–10). From time to time there were outbreaks of violence and those involved were brutally crushed (see the reference in Luke 13:1 to the "Galileans whose blood Pilate had mingled with the blood of their sacrifices"). Although during the time of Jesus these difficult economic and social conditions caused tension, they did not yet boil into revolt as it happened later. However, the people at the time of Jesus did experience tension, fear, and, on occasion, brutal violence. The Gospels portray Jesus as a healer—a ministry that not only relieved those who suffered from physical pain and limitation, but also represented the healing of a people scarred by violence and in danger of losing their identity and dignity, a people subjugated by demonic powers.

In the Gospels we see Jesus' mission as a great liberation and restoration of the people, lifting them out of darkness and bringing new life and dignity. The keynote of Jesus' mission—particularly as presented in the synoptic Gospels—was the advent of the Kingdom or Reign of God, a Jewish hope that God would bring life and lasting peace to Israel where all human efforts in the past had proved bankrupt. Jesus brought this Good News in an urgent way especially to those who were confined to the fringes of society: the sick and the poor. He gathered a community of disciples and gave them a share in his liberating mission. He challenged the wealthy and the religious authorities and, in the spirit of the great prophets of the Old Testament, predicted that God would reverse the fortunes of the poor and the powerful and restore justice. He revered the Law of Moses and the Scriptures of the Old Testament, but his interpretation of the Law was guided unerringly by its central command of love of God and neighbor (Matthew 22:34–40)—a focus that was viewed by some of the religious authorities as too lax.

Although the Gospels accurately report that Jesus' messianic mission was primarily confined to the region of Israel and that he had few encounters with Gentiles, those that are included demonstrate Jesus' openness to Gentiles, such as the centurion of Capernaum (Matthew 8:5–13), the Gerasene demoniac (Mark 5:1–20), and, after some persuasion, the Canaanite woman from Tyre and Sidon (Mark 7:24–30 and Matthew 15:21–28). In Luke's Gospel Jesus challenges his hometown congregation in Nazareth by recalling the mission of Elijah to the widow in the region of Tyre and Sidon and the willingness of Elisha to heal Naaman the Syrian (Luke 4:25–27), harbingers of the early Christian community's movement out into the Gentile world.

No doubt this motif of Jesus' inclusive mission, coupled with the compelling power of his teaching, the magnetism of his charismatic healings, and his challenges to the inequities and hypocrisy of the ruling powers raised deadly opposition to Jesus and led ultimately to his arrest, trial, and crucifixion in Jerusalem. For his Jewish opponents, Jesus was a dangerous threat to public order and to their own religious authority—one who seemed to relativize important strictures of the Mosaic Law. The Romans, on their part, were alert to any signs of rebellion, signs only too visible in both the agitation of the Jewish authorities about Jesus and in the public disturbances caused by his dramatic appearance in Jerusalem and its Temple.

From Jesus to the Post-Resurrection Community

Each of the Gospels concludes with an account of Jesus' Death and Resurrection, for Jesus' mission of healing and teaching, his fearless confrontation with evil, and his prophetic challenges ultimately led to his Death. In this sense, the Death of Jesus was the final expression of his life-giving service that had characterized his mission in Galilee and Judea. Coupled with the terrible reality of Jesus' Death by crucifixion was his triumph over death, as God raised Jesus from the prison of his tomb and exalted him as the Son of God and Savior of the world. That triumph over death through Resurrection was the catalyst for full Christian faith. His disciples, who had been disillusioned and scattered under the impact of the Death of Jesus, were reconciled and reconstituted as the community of Jesus through a series of post-Resurrection appearances and ecstatic visions. Through the power of the Spirit lavished on this community by the Risen Christ, the disciples took up the mission of Jesus and ultimately brought it to the wider world.

The beginning of the post-Easter community and its mission is the fundamental story proclaimed in the Acts of the Apostles, a kind of sequel to the Gospel according to Luke.[4] The formula expressed in the Risen Christ's final words to his disciples guides the overall structure of that New Testament book: "But you will receive power when the holy Spirit comes upon you, and you will be my witnesses in Jerusalem, throughout Judea and Samaria, and to the ends of the earth" (Acts 1:8; see also Luke 24:47–48). As commanded by the Risen Christ, the early Christian missionaries would gradually bring the Gospel to the wider Mediterranean world.

---

4   See chapter 6, pages 72–92.

CHAPTER 4

The History of the New Testament: From Jesus to Paul

The profound impact of the Resurrection of Christ on those who believed in him and the rapid spread of the Christian community set up the context in which Paul the Apostle came on the scene. The earliest Christian community was composed of Jews who believed in Jesus as the Messiah and Son of God. They ascribed to the Risen Christ a religious identity and authority without precedent within the traditions of Judaism. Gradually, in the inclusive and generous spirit of Jesus' own mission, they took the Gospel beyond the confines of Israel and began to incorporate Gentiles within their communities. The early Church came to believe that the mission to the Gentiles was, in fact, the ultimate plan of God, a fulfillment and expansion of Israel's own role as God's Chosen People. The Acts of the Apostles affirms that the Gospel would begin to spread to Samaria—an area Jews considered outside the bonds of orthodox faith—to Ethiopia, to Roman soldiers such as Cornelius of Caesarea Maritima, and to the Greeks in Antioch and beyond.

Although on one level the Acts of the Apostles seems to present the worldwide mission of the early Church as an inevitable force, in fact the early Jewish Christians struggled to grasp the full scope of their God-given mission and had to make adjustments—sometimes reluctantly—in their customs and ways of life in order to make space for Gentile converts. The Jewish Christian leaders of Jerusalem are shocked when Peter baptizes the Roman officer, Cornelius, and his whole household, and call him on the carpet to explain. Only after they hear Peter's testimony that these Gentiles had been gifted with the Holy Spirit do the leaders agree (see Act 11:18). Later the same group of Jerusalem leaders is nervous when they hear that some missionaries had baptized Gentiles in Antioch, and they send Barnabas, one of the most trusted leaders of the early Church, to see what is going on (Acts 11:19–26). And we know from the testimony of Paul's letters that his own mission to the Gentiles was criticized and even undermined by Jewish Christians who thought that only Gentiles who first converted to Judaism could become Christians. Paul also confronted Peter when the former heard reports that the leader of the Apostles had withdrawn from table fellowship with Gentiles in Antioch under the pressure of criticism from Jewish Christians in Jerusalem (Galatians 2:11–14).

This struggle of the early Jewish Christian movement to navigate the transition from a Church that was completely Jewish in character to one increasingly Gentile in makeup helps put the mission of Paul in perspective. Paul was born early in the first century, probably a few years after the birth of Jesus, in Tarsus (Acts 22:3), a university town in south central Asia Minor. Apparently he spent time studying Jewish tradition in Jerusalem under the famous teacher Gamaliel (Acts 5:34). In Acts, Paul also claims to be a naturally born Roman citizen (22:25–29). At first Paul, himself a devout Jew, fiercely opposed this new movement (see Paul's own testimony to this in Galatians 1:13 and Philippians 3:6). He approves of the stoning of Stephen, the first martyr of the early Church (see Acts 7:58, in which Paul even guards the cloaks of those who throw the stones). He gains authorization from the religious authorities to haul Christians to prison, including women and children. We do not know for sure Paul's reasons for such opposition. By his own admission, Paul was a strict Jew and one "zealous" for the tradition of his ancestors (see Galatians 1:14). Perhaps he considered this emerging movement of the followers of Jesus to be too liberal in their interpretation of the Law. Perhaps

> By his own admission, Paul was a strict Jew and one "zealous" for the tradition of his ancestors.

he, like many others, was shocked and scandalized that fellow Jews would dare to acclaim a crucified and accursed criminal as God's Messiah—something that had not been anticipated in the Old Testament or Jewish tradition.[1] Perhaps in a period when the cohesion of Judaism as one people was under threat he believed that the growing strength of the followers of Jesus and their inclusion of non-Jews would be divisive and further weaken the unity of his people.

In any case, Paul went on to experience a profound and lasting transformation of his view of Jesus and his followers. The Acts of the Apostles portrays this happening in a dramatic fashion while he is on his way to Damascus to attack Christians. Paul has a vision of the Risen Christ that stops him in his tracks: "Saul, Saul, why are you persecuting me?" (Acts 9:4). The Risen Christ was truly present

> Within a few days, according to Acts, Paul began his preaching career in the local synagogues.

in the vulnerable community of believers that Paul was attempting to destroy. The now-dazed Paul was led into Damascus where a local Christian, Ananias, healed him from his blindness and where within a few days, according to Acts, Paul began his preaching career in the local synagogues. Some years later, Paul himself reflected on this inaugural experience in his Letter to the Galatians, describing this reception of a "revelation of Jesus Christ" in less dramatic but still profound terms as awaking to a call from God, a call that set Paul apart even before his conception in his mother's womb (Galatians 1:11–17).

Through this remarkable personal experience of the Risen Christ, Paul fearlessly proclaimed that the Crucified Christ was indeed the promised Messiah and ardently defended the mission to the Gentiles, the very things that earlier he had fiercely opposed. Even the Acts of the Apostles concedes that Paul's quick turnaround from persecutor to Apostle was astounding to the Jewish Christians

---

1 Later Christian interpreters found antecedents for the sufferings of Christ in traditions such as the Suffering Servant of Isaiah or the suffering just one in the Book of Wisdom, but in Jewish tradition these figures were not identified with the Messiah.

of Jerusalem. When Paul comes to visit, Acts notes, "they were all afraid of him, not believing that he was a disciple" (Acts 9:26).

Antioch and the Launch of Paul's Missionary Journeys

Paul's passionate preaching in Jerusalem and the controversy it caused there prompted the Jewish Christian community to send Paul back to his home town of Tarsus out of fear for his safety. That sojourn, or "exile," turned out to be the preface to Paul's extraordinary missionary career. According to the Acts of the Apostles, the ever-faithful and gracious mediator Barnabas was instrumental in bringing Paul back into the picture. He took Paul to Antioch where there was now a vibrant Christian community, composed of both Jewish and Gentile Christians. There we can assume that Paul, under the tutelage of Barnabas and other Christians, would be more deeply formed in the Christian "Way."[2] Paul, we might note, insisted at times that he received his grounding in the Christian faith directly from the Risen Christ and had conferred only briefly with the leaders of the Church (see Galatians 1:18–20), but in fact Paul also confesses that he was the recipient of important Christian traditions and depended on such traditions (see, for example, 1 Corinthians 11:23 concerning the Lord's Supper and 1 Corinthians 15:3 concerning the Resurrection).

Antioch was the base for the early Christian mission to the west. From there Paul, in the company of Barnabas, John Mark, and later Silvanus (Silas) and Timothy and others, began the remarkable series of missionary expeditions into Asia Minor, and later into Macedonia, and then the Greek province of Achaia. Subsequently Paul would retrace his steps in this region, revisiting the communities he had evangelized. Some historians estimate that Paul traveled

---

2   In the Acts of the Apostles, Luke indicates that the early Christians designated themselves as the people of the Way (see 9:2; 18:25; 19:9, 23; 22:4). In Antioch the followers of Jesus were first called "Christians" by outsiders (Acts 11:26).

nearly ten thousand miles during his missionary career, some of it by sea, but much of it on foot. Although the precise time frame of Paul's missionary career—and the exact dates of his individual letters—are still debated, it is likely that Paul began his missionary journeys around AD 37 or 38. The Acts of the Apostles notes that Paul was in Corinth when Gallio was proconsul of the southern Greek province of Achaia (Acts 18:12–16). An inscription found in the Greek city of Delphi dates Gallio's terms of service as AD 51–52, and this date has served as something of a marker for estimating the rest of Paul's chronology. Based on that fixed date, most scholars estimate that Paul's missionary career lasted some twenty-five to thirty years, ending with his martyrdom in Rome under Nero, sometime around AD 64–68. Acts concludes with Paul reaching Rome, the imperial capital, but on a prison ship and enduring house arrest (Acts, chapters 27—28). Paul himself had spoken of wishing to go on to Spain, the far eastern boundary of the Roman Empire, (see Romans 15:24) but it appears that his martyrdom prevented the fulfillment of this hope.

> Most scholars estimate that Paul's missionary career lasted some twenty-five to thirty years, ending with his martyrdom in Rome.

Paul's Missionary Method and the Role of His Letters

To understand the purpose and nature of Paul's letters we should first consider the circumstances in which his mission took shape. From both the testimony of Acts and indications in Paul's own letters, his first step after arriving at a new location was to visit the local synagogue. Paul's assumption at the outset was that his fellow Jews would be as moved by the message of the Gospel as he was. In many of the diaspora synagogues, the Jewish congregation would be joined on a regular basis by Gentile admirers who had deep respect for Judaism as an ancient religion and for the clarity and strength of its ethical teaching. Most of these Gentiles would not convert to Judaism but were well informed about its Scriptures and its traditions. In many cases, these Gentile "God-fearers," as they were known, would respond more favorably to Paul's message than the Jewish members of the congregation—some of whom would resent Paul's message and the disruption his appeal would have. Paul would be hounded by these opponents, as both the stories in Acts and Paul's own comments in his letters attest.[3] The God-fearers who responded to Paul's message, along with Jews who also were persuaded by Paul, ultimately formed the nucleus of these early Christian communities. Paul did not consider his role to be the leader of the local communities he evangelized. As Paul put it, "According to the grace of God given to me, like a wise master builder I laid a foundation, and another is building upon it" (1 Corinthians 3:10). In some instances, there were already local leaders in place, such as the Jewish Christian couple, Aquila and Priscilla, in Corinth (Acts 18:2–3; they later became important coworkers with Paul in Ephesus). In other cases, Paul would designate elders to serve as leaders. After a relatively short time, Paul would move on to his next destination, although by exception he spent almost two years in Ephesus, part of it in prison.

Paul the Letter Writer

This itinerant quality to Paul's missionary work sets the stage for his letters, which are extensions of his missionary program. In some instances, such as the First Letter to the Thessalonians (which is probably the earliest New Testament writing we have), Paul writes because he is anxious to know how this community is faring after he had to leave prematurely (Acts 17:1–10). Paul confesses that he had hoped to get back to them more than once but has been thwarted in his plans to do so; instead he sends Timothy as his emissary and when, upon Timothy's return, he receives word that all is well in

---

3   See, for example, the disturbance in Thessalonica where Paul's preaching causes a division in the synagogue: Acts 17:1–8.

Thessalonica, Paul is overjoyed and decides to write this letter to express his gratitude (see 1 Thessalonians 2:17—3:8). But in doing so, Paul also responds to some questions that the community there had about the fate of their fellow Christians who had died before the final coming of Christ. What would be their fate, they had asked Paul (probably a question sent along with Timothy). Paul uses the letter to respond to this poignant pastoral question, reassuring the Christians there that their beloved dead would not be deprived of the joy of Christ's return because they had died before that time.

In another instance, Paul writes what could be considered primarily a letter of personal recommendation. This is the case with the Letter to Philemon, the briefest Pauline letter, but also one of the most enticing. In this case Paul addresses Philemon, a leader of a local Christian community, and pleads on behalf of Onesimus, probably a runaway slave whom Paul has befriended in prison. He now asks the master, Philemon, to be reconciled with Onesimus because he is a fellow Christian. While the immediate purpose of the letter is to persuade Philemon about this, Paul also uses the occasion to make the point that the bonds of love and concern among Christians take priority over any legal rights Philemon might have to punish his wayward slave—no doubt a teaching not only for Philemon to consider but also for the "church at your house" (Philemon 2).

Most of Paul's letters are addressed to congregations and are either prompted by a situation that concerns Paul (for example, the backsliding of the Galatians under the pressure of strict Jewish Christians, or the divisions among some leaders of the community at Philippi) or because of specific pastoral issues that have been posed for Paul by members of the community (as for example, the long laundry list of problems and pastoral issues in 1 Corinthians). Note, too, that in many instances Paul cowrites his letters with some of his fellow missionaries, such as Timothy (2 Corinthians 1:1; Philippians 1:1; 1 Thessalonians 1:1; 2 Thessalonians 1:1; Philemon 1:1), Silvanus, sometimes known as Silas (1 Thessalonians 1:1; 2 Thessalonians 1:1) and Sosthenes (1 Corinthians 1:1). It is also likely that Paul dictated his letters to one or more secretaries, who probably had to write furiously to keep up with Paul's passionate prose. In one instance, Paul seems to grab the pen himself and makes an important point he wants to emphasize: "See with what large letters I am writing to you in my own hand!" (Galatians 6:11; see also Colossians 4:18).

Thus both by personal emissaries and through his letters, Paul maintained contact with his communities and also helped advance their Christian formation. Paul was not a "lone ranger," but worked in collaboration with a wide network of fellow missionaries and local community leaders. In the conclusion to his letter to Rome, a community that Paul had not visited and did not found, he gives personal greetings to a long list of personal friends and apostolic associates. These are apparently men and women he knows there from his wide-ranging apostolic work, including Phoebe, the deacon of the Corinthian port city of Cenchreae, who is probably the bearer of Paul's letter to Rome and whom Paul praises as "our sister . . . who has been a benefactor to many and to me as well" (see Romans 16:1–23).

It is likely that Paul dictated his letters to one or more secretaries, who probably had to write furiously to keep up with Paul's passionate prose.

The Format and Number of Paul's Letters

Paul uses the general format of letter writing common in the Greco-Roman world of his day. His letter to the Philippians is a good example:

1. Letters would typically begin by identifying the sender and the recipient: "Paul and Timothy, slaves of Christ Jesus, to all the holy ones in Christ Jesus who are in Philippi, with the overseers and ministers" (Philippians 1:1).

2. Next would come a greeting: "Grace to you and peace from God our Father and the Lord Jesus Christ" (Philippians 1:2).

3. In Paul's case, the greeting was usually followed by a prayer of thanksgiving, like the beautiful one in this letter to a community

Paul especially cares for. It begins: "I give thanks to my God at every remembrance of you . . ." (Philippians 1:3–11).

4. Then would follow the body of the letter (Philippians 1:12—4:23). In the case of Philippians, Paul turns first to assuring them about his ongoing ministry of proclaiming the Gospel despite his imprisonment and other opposition (Philippians 1:12), and then he takes up other issues such as his concerns about divisions in the community.

5. The conclusion would usually include any final requests and some specific farewells. In the case of Philippians, the farewell is rather brief: "Give my greetings to every holy one in Christ Jesus. The brothers who are with me send you their greetings; all the holy ones send you their greetings, especially those of Caesar's household. The grace of the Lord Jesus Christ be with your spirit" (Philippians 4:21–23).

The use of this conventional format and the style of Paul's letters suggest that he was well-schooled in basic rhetoric. He uses a number of typical forms of argumentation and persuasion found in the writings of this period. While Paul was not a scholar, he was educated and used this background in his apostolic work. Paul did not hesitate to freely adapt the conventional letter format, incorporating liturgical blessings, prayers, and hymns into his communications with his communities. Such is the case with the Letter to the Philippians, where Paul seems to insert an early Christian hymn (Philippians 2:6–11). In beautiful images it asserts that Christ "emptied himself" and it speaks of him "taking the form of a slave." The hymn bolsters Paul's plea that the Philippians avoid divisions and disputes and instead take on the humble and gracious attitude of Jesus himself (Philippians 2:3).

Which Letters Did Paul Write?

Scholars continue to debate whether all the letters traditionally listed as composed by Paul should in fact be attributed directly to Paul himself or whether they were written later by a disciple of Paul. There is strong consensus on the seven undisputed letters of Paul: Romans, 1 and 2 Corinthians, Galatians, Philippians, 1 Thessalonians, and Philemon. Yet scholars are divided about whether Colossians and 2 Thessalonians were written by Paul or a later author. Some believe that the vocabulary and theological perspectives of these letters indicate that they, too, were composed by a later disciple of Paul rather than by the Apostle himself. For example, where Paul in 1 Corinthians spoke of the Church as "Christ's body," composed of many members (1 Corinthians 12), Colossians refers to Christ as the "head" of the Body that is the Church (see, for example, Colossians 1:18). And Colossians is concerned about the lordship of Christ over the principalities and powers of the universe (Colossians 2:15–20), a cosmic perspective not emphasized by Paul himself.

Many scholars question whether Ephesians was written by Paul or if it was a letter at all. The reference to "in Ephesus" in the greeting is missing in several ancient manuscripts and the overall format does not have the usual characteristics of a Pauline letter. Some suggest that Ephesians may be a kind of summary of Paul's thought that was circulated among the various local churches sometime after Paul's life. A majority of scholars assign the so-called "pastoral letters" of 1 and 2 Timothy and Titus to a period later in the first century when concerns about Church structure and the maintenance of sound tradition arose.[4]

The question of the "authenticity" of some Pauline letters should not be exaggerated. In any case, all of these letters are part of the Church's Scriptures and were so from the earliest centuries. In most instances scholars who doubt whether Paul actually composed these writings, concede that these letters are extensions of Paul's theology into new circumstances by those who knew and revered Paul's teaching. Thus

In any case, all of these letters are part of the Church's Scriptures and were so from the earliest centuries.

---

4 On Hebrews, see the section at the end of this chapter.

these letters are designated as "deutero-Pauline" letters (that is, in a secondary, somewhat removed category), another example of what we saw in the Old Testament, where earlier traditions are maintained and reinterpreted by later generations.

Determining the chronological order of Paul's letters is even more difficult than deciding authorship. One thing is clear, the order of Paul's letters in the New Testament canon is not a chronological order; the Letter to the Romans, which is listed first (probably because of its length) is most likely the one written last. Listed eighth in order, 1 Thessalonians was probably the first one to be written.

A possible sequencing of Paul's letters suggested by many scholars would be as follows:

1. First Letter to the Thessalonians, written about AD 50 from Corinth, after Timothy brought news of the Thessalonians, as Acts 18:5 and Paul himself indicate (1 Thessalonians 3:6–8).

2. Letter to the Galatians, written around AD 53, probably from Ephesus, to a group of churches in the area of central Asia Minor.

3. First Letter to the Corinthians, written shortly after Galatians, also likely from Ephesus where Paul resided for two years, spending a portion of that time in prison (1 Corinthians 15:32).

4. Philippians, written around AD 55, probably also from Ephesus and from prison (Philippians 1:12–13).

5. Philemon, the briefest of Paul's letters written from prison to Philemon, the leader of a house church in Colossae, probably around AD 55. Onesimus, the slave referred to in this letter, is mentioned in Colossians 4:9 as being from that city; Archippus, to whom the letter is also addressed, is mentioned both in Colossians (4:17) and in Philemon 2. Paul may be writing from prison in Ephesus, although other scholars prefer Rome—the latter case would put the Letter to Philemon near the end of Paul's life.

6. Second Letter to the Corinthians, which may be a merger of two or more letters, was probably composed sometime around AD 55–56, again most likely during Paul's sojourn in Ephesus.

7. Romans was probably the last of Paul's letters, possibly written from Corinth around AD 57 when Paul made his last visit to this city. Paul had not yet visited Rome, and in writing to the community in this key city he makes the letter something of a summation of his fundamental Christian vision.

The other deutero-Pauline letters such as Ephesians, Colossians, and 2 Thessalonians, and the pastoral letters of 1 and 2 Timothy and Titus were probably written in the last quarter of the first century. Some interpreters date the pastoral letters even to the beginning of the second century.

The Letters of Paul and the Life of the Early Christian Communities

As we have noted, Paul's letters were not written in a vacuum, but were an integral part of his apostolic mission. It is interesting that most of the letters were written in the latter part of Paul's missionary career and benefited from the rich apostolic experience he had gained by that time. By reading closely the entire span of his letters we can piece together his theology. Paul does not refer in much detail to the circumstances of Jesus' life, although he does note his human birth (Galatians 4:4), his celebration of a final Passover with his disciples (1 Corinthians 11:23–25), and his suffering and crucifixion (1 Corinthians 2:8; 15:3–4). He does explicitly convey Jesus' teaching about divorce (1 Corinthians 7:10) and, most importantly, the absolute centrality of the love command in Jesus' teaching (1 Corinthians 13:1–13; Galatians 5:6). Instead of presenting many biographical details about Jesus, Paul focused in a laser-like way on the central defining acts of Jesus' God-given mission—namely his Death and Resurrection, the "Paschal mystery." There can be little doubt that Paul was shaped by the impact of Jesus and his mission that was transmitted in the witness and collective memory of the early Church.

Paul's letters reveal his broad and deep Christian vision: his profound understanding of the God of Israel, a gift of his Jewish heritage, and one deepened and illumined by his encounter with the Risen Christ; his ardent relationship with the Crucified Christ and his realization of the awesome identity of Jesus as Son of God and Savior of the world; his view of the destiny of the human person as a new creation in Christ and of the community of Christians bound together as one Body of Christ and gifted by the Spirit. We hear his insistent message that the grace of God was to be lavished not only on his beloved Israel but on the entire world. We also witness Paul's unyielding commitment to his vocation as Apostle to the Gentiles and his strong hope that never dimmed despite the sufferings he had to endure.

What Paul communicated to his communities was not a pre-packaged set of teachings that he simply handed on to them. Rather, much of Paul's understanding of God and of Christ and of what it means to be a follower of Christ was fashioned in dialogue with his fellow Christians. Their testimonies of faith (that he praises so generously in letters such as 1 Thessalonians and Philippians), the traditions that the Apostles and other leaders maintained, the communities' struggles, their questions posed to him, even their failures and problems—all of these drew from Paul the eloquent and challenging message of his letters. We learn from Paul's letters that they were sent to the communities in the hands of trusted coworkers. And we can be sure that those who bore these letters were also present when they were read to the congregations addressed. The bearers of the letters may, in fact, have been their readers and, no doubt, offered words of further explanation about Paul's meaning and engaged in discussion with the Christians gathered to hear them.

Further, we can confidently assume that the settings in which Paul's letters were read and heard were not casual gatherings, but almost surely in a setting where the community had gathered for

We can be sure that those who bore these letters were also present when they were read to the congregations addressed.

prayer and Eucharist. Paul would realize this, and most of his letters reflect the liturgical setting in which they would be proclaimed. He incorporates beautiful words of thanksgiving, includes snatches of hymns, and from time to time he breaks into praise of God's glory. Thus the place that the letters of Paul have in our Eucharist today, with segments of them read from the Lectionary during the Liturgy of the Word, is in direct continuity with the very origin and purpose of Paul's writings.

Conclusion: Christ Proclaimed— by Letters and Gospels

Thus the first New Testament writings come from Paul the Apostle. Like all of the New Testament writings, Paul's letters, similar to his preaching, were rooted in the life and ministry of Jesus, viewed against the backdrop of the Old Testament. Although Paul's medium of expression—letters—would necessarily be different than the narrative style of the Gospels, both Paul and the Evangelists proclaim the same Christ, the one whom John's Gospel would describe as the "Word made flesh," the Word "spoken" by God whose unconditional love wished not to condemn the world but to save it. Paul, therefore, was neither the "founder" of Christianity, as some interpreters have claimed, nor did his different style of proclamation distort the community's memory of who Jesus truly was. He was God's trumpet, who proclaimed the Gospel of Jesus Christ to the world.

Postscript: The Letter to the Hebrews

The authorship of the Letter to the Hebrews has been contested from the early centuries of the Church. The church of Alexandria, the possible place of the letter's origin, considered it an authentic letter of Paul, but this was debated in the churches of the West. Modern biblical scholarship is virtually unanimous in not assigning this letter to Paul. The title "to the Hebrews" is not part of the text itself; it was attached in the early manuscripts and probably implies that the intended audience was Jewish Christians. In fact, Hebrews is not really a letter, as it lacks the usual opening identification of the author or a greeting and is more precisely identified as a fervent exhortation to the Christians addressed to remain faithful in spite of duress. In its conclusion, however, Hebrews refers to "our brother Timothy" (13:23) and sends greetings from "those from Italy" (13:24). That concluding greeting probably refers to Christians in Alexandria who were originally from Italy.

What calls into question Pauline authorship is the unique style and theological perspective of this beautifully written letter. The author develops an elaborate metaphor to describe the redemptive work of Christ. Drawing on neo-Platonic thought that saw earthly realities as mere shadows of the heavenly realities, the author contrasts the sacrifice of Christ's Death with the sacrifices of the Jerusalem Temple, particularly on the Day of Atonement when the high priest alone would enter the Temple's inner sanctuary. Jesus is portrayed as the true "High Priest" whose sacrifice is once for all and completely efficacious—he enters, first among all creation, into the true heavenly sanctuary. This assurance of salvation through the Death and exaltation of Christ on our behalf leads to the final section of the letter, and its ultimate purpose, where the author urges the Christians to persevere, as the saints of old did, and to be confident of their entrance into the heavenly sanctuary and thus into the presence of God.

CHAPTER 5

The History of the New Testament: From Jesus to the Gospels

The four Gospels appear first in the sequence of books that make up the New Testament canon because they focus on the person and ministry of Jesus, which is the foundation for all of Christian faith.[1] But the Gospels are neither raw chronicles of the life of Jesus, nor were they written during his lifetime but several decades after his Death and Resurrection. These four narratives are "proclamation"—the preaching of the Good News about Jesus and his mission of bringing God's redemptive love to the world. The very term "Gospel" from the Greek word *euangelion* literally means "good news"; its etymology is traced back to experiences where good news was publicly announced and celebrated after a victory in battle or deliverance from some threatening calamity. A famous text from Isaiah 52:7 (quoted by Paul in Romans 10:15) captures the exuberant meaning of the term: "How beautiful upon the mountains / are the feet of the one bringing good news" (the word *euangelion* in the Greek version).

Paul himself uses both the noun ("the gospel") and the verb form of *euangelion* ("to preach the gospel") frequently in his letters. For Paul the term does not apply to narratives about Jesus' life, but to the Apostles' preaching about Jesus. The opening verse of Mark's Gospel may be the first to apply the term to the story of Jesus' life: "The beginning of the gospel of Jesus Christ [the Son of God]" (Mark

---

1   On the formation of the canon see chapter 8, pages 100–117.

1:1), but even here the evangelist may intend to say that the narrative about Jesus that follows is the "beginning" or foundation of Christian proclamation. To be equipped to preach the Good News, one has to experience Jesus, Crucified and Risen, as the first disciples did. In fact, Paul uses this identical phrase—"the beginning of the gospel"—to refer to the beginning of his missionary career when the Philippians came to his aid (Philippians 4:15).

The term "Gospel" was applied to the work of the four evangelists only in the second century, mentioned by St. Justin Martyr, writing about AD 155. Yet it is a very apt term since these prime New Testament books were meant to be "preaching"; that is, proclaiming in narrative form the Good News of Jesus Christ. To do that, the Gospels drew on the early Christian community's collective memory of Jesus' public ministry, now understood more profoundly under the impact of the Resurrection of Jesus and the outpouring of the Holy Spirit on the post-Easter community. The Jesus who lived, died, and triumphed over death in Roman Palestine in the first third of the first century was now made present as the Risen Christ to the post-Easter communities that went on to hear and experience the Gospel narratives.

The Three-Stage Process Leading to the Gospels

Recent Catholic teaching has provided a way of understanding the process that led from the actual time of Jesus' ministry to the composition of the four Gospels. In 1964, the Pontifical Biblical Commission, a Vatican advisory committee appointed by the pope, published a document titled "Instruction on the Historical Truth of the Gospels." In it the Commission proposed that the Gospels were formed in a three-stage historical process.[2] The Commission's document appeared while the Second Vatican Council was still going on. In the final session

---

2   Pontifical Biblical Commission, *Instruction on the Historical Truth of the Gospels* (Rome, 1964).

of the Council (fall 1965), this same view of the Gospels' formation was incorporated into one of the Council's major documents, the *Dogmatic Constitution on Divine Revelation*, also known by the first two Latin words of the text, *Dei Verbum* ("the Word of God"). In his beautiful 2010 reflection on the role of the Scriptures in the life and ministry of the Church, Pope Benedict XVI also drew on this body of teaching.[3]

While explicitly formulated in these modern Church documents, this same basic process was already expressed in Luke's prologue to his Gospel account. There he briefs "Theophilus" (either a benefactor or perhaps a real or symbolic person to whom he dedicates his two-volume work) on the purpose of what he has written and refers to a chain of tradition originating with "eyewitnesses from the beginning," then "the ministers of the word," and then "I [Luke] too have decided . . . to write it down in an orderly sequence . . ." (Luke 1:1–4). Thus Luke's Gospel stands at the end of a process that began with the testimony of eyewitnesses to Jesus, was carried forward in the early decades of the Church by "ministers of the word," and was then shaped into a full Gospel narrative by Luke.

1. Jesus and His Disciples: Experiencing the Life, Mission, Death, and Resurrection of Christ

The focus of the Gospel accounts is, of course, the life and ministry of Jesus of Nazareth, and the climax of that mission in his Passion, Death, and Resurrection. We have briefly described the fundamental components of Jesus' mission in the previous chapter.[4] In diverse ways, the four Gospels portray Jesus' urgent ministry of teaching—often in the form of his interpretation of the Law of Moses—his passionate healing, his outreach to those on the margins of society, his emphasis in word and deed on the love command, and his sharp confrontations with the religious authorities who opposed his mission. Jesus' keynote announcement of the coming Reign of God and the

---

3   Benedict XVI, *The Word of the Lord (Verbum Domini)*, Postsynodal Apostolic Exhortation. (2010).

4   See chapter 3, pages 38–44.

challenging impact of his mission led to growing opposition and ultimately to his condemnation by the religious authorities in Jerusalem, his public execution by the Romans under the jurisdiction of Pontius Pilate, and his burial. The actual moment of Jesus' Resurrection is not described in the Gospel accounts, but they do note its profound *impact* on his disciples through the discovery of the empty tomb and several appearances to the disciples by the Risen Christ.

The followers of Jesus did not produce written accounts of Jesus during his lifetime, at least none are referred to in the New Testament, nor has any evidence of such texts ever been found. What did happen, especially under the impact of the Resurrection, was that the person and mission of Jesus had profound consequences for his followers, changing their lives forever. The overall experience of Jesus left a deep impression on the collective consciousness of the earliest group of disciples, an impression fueled by their encounters with the Risen Christ. That impression was indelible and life-changing. Disciples who huddled in fear or decided to walk away in despair after the arrest and Crucifixion of Jesus, were transformed by these visionary and ecstatic experiences into bold witnesses and heroic proclaimers of the Good News. The first stage of the Gospel process, then, originates both in the actual historical life and ministry of Jesus of Nazareth, his selfless Death, and the triumph of his Resurrection, as well as in the experience, memory, and witness of Jesus' earliest followers.

2. The Disciples and the Early Church: Sustaining Jesus' Memory in Communities of Faith

The witness of the earliest followers of Jesus and their proclamation of the "Good News" about him lead into the second stage in the formation of the Gospel accounts. This period would extend from about the year AD 30, following the Death and Resurrection of Jesus, up to about AD 70, marked by the destruction of the Jerusalem Temple and the significant impact it had on both Judaism and early Christianity.

Paul's own missionary efforts and the story of the early Church narrated in the Acts of the Apostles give us an idea of this dynamic period. Emboldened by the Holy Spirit, the Apostles begin to proclaim Jesus' Resurrection and to heal in his name (see the first such story of Peter's healing of the paralyzed man at the Temple gate in Acts 3:1–10). As time went on and the apostolic group began to realize the full scope of the mission entrusted to them by the Risen Christ, they took it beyond the confines of Israel and it began to take hold in places such as northern Africa, the eastern Arabian Peninsula, the island of Cyprus, then to Antioch and Asia Minor, and on to Macedonia, mainland Greece, and around the Mediterranean rim to Rome.

There is also evidence that the Christian movement spread, not always by the outward thrust of apostolic preaching, but also because Gentiles wanted to come into the community. In the Gospels most of the Gentile characters approach Jesus rather than the other way around: for example, the centurion in Capernaum (Matthew 8:5–13), the Gerasene demoniac (Mark 5:1–20), the Syrophoenician woman from Tyre and Sidon (Mark 7:24–30), certain "Greeks" who wish to see Jesus in John's Gospel (John 12:20–21), and in Matthew's account, the Magi who come to seek out the infant Jesus (Matthew 2:1–12). These Gospel stories may anticipate the later experience of the community in which Gentiles sought to belong; Gentiles such as the "God-fearers" who frequented the synagogues[5] and responded to Paul's preaching, and others who had witnessed the cohesion and joy of the early Christian communities.[6]

The Christian message was kept alive through the various activities of the early Christian community. In their missionary preaching, the Apostles and other early witnesses surely invoked stories about the life and teaching of Jesus. These gatherings of the Christians for prayer and celebrations of the Eucharist were certainly

> In the Gospels most of the Gentile characters approach Jesus rather than the other way around.

---

5   Concerning God-fearers, see chapter 4, pages 49–50.

6   On this, see Rodney Stark, *The Rise of Christianity: A Sociologist Reconsiders History* (Princeton: Princeton University Press, 1996).

a prime context in which the Gospel material was heard and explained. Most of these assemblies would be in private homes or in workshops or other modest spaces. In larger Roman villas, perhaps thirty or forty Christians could gather for worship, followed by a common meal shared together.[7] Paul alludes more than once to such house churches (1 Corinthians 1:11–17; 11:17–21; Philemon 1). The Acts of the Apostles describes the Jerusalem Christians gathering in their homes for fellowship and prayer and going together to the Temple to offer worship (Acts 2:42–47).

Who were the bearers of this "Good News"? It makes sense that the first generation of those who walked with Jesus and knew him personally would be revered by the early Christians. People would be eager to hear their eyewitness accounts about Jesus. Paul, for example, refers both to the Apostles and many other witnesses in this first generation (1 Corinthians 15:5–11). He refers to himself somewhat wistfully as "one born abnormally" (1 Corinthians 15:8), since he had been blessed with a visionary experience of the Risen Christ but had not personally known Jesus of Nazareth during his lifetime. This generation of eyewitnesses ultimately passed from the scene and other Spirit-filled teachers and preachers carried the Gospel tradition during this intermediary period. The Didache, an early Christian text from the latter part of the first century, refers to itinerant Christian "prophets" who circulated among the local churches preaching the Gospel. The Acts of the Apostles tells us of Apollos, a zealous convert from Alexandria, who was preaching in Asia Minor and Greece. While at Ephesus he is taken under the wing of Paul's friends and coworkers, Priscilla and Aquila. While giving him further instruction in the Christian "way," they learn that he was familiar only with the baptism of John (Acts

> People would be eager to hear the eyewitness accounts about Jesus.

---

7   This is the estimate of Jerome Murphy-O'Connor after measuring the available space in the remains of some Roman villas in Corinth; see *St. Paul's Corinth: Texts and Archaeology* (Collegeville, MN: Liturgical Press, 2002), 178–185.

18:24–28). Later, Apollos went to Corinth to minister and is mentioned in Paul's First Letter to the Corinthians (1 Corinthians 1:12; 3:5, 22; 16:12). We can also assume that many of those who hosted the gatherings of Christians in their homes also took an active role in maintaining the Gospel tradition. In his graceful letter to Philemon Paul refers to him as "our beloved and our co-worker" and also mentions "our sister" Apphia and "our fellow soldier" Archippus, all of whom were probably significant leaders in this house church (Philemon 1–2).

To a certain extent, this collective memory of the early community was selective. The intent was not to keep a complete historical record about Jesus, but to remember in a special way those aspects of his life that nourished the faith of the early believers—inspiring them, instructing them, and challenging them to follow in the way of Jesus. Thus we learn little about Jesus' physical appearance or the tone of his voice, and there are long gaps in the accounts of his life, such as the period from his childhood to the beginning of his public ministry. Some of this information was probably lost with the deaths of the earliest eyewitnesses. The narrator of John's Gospel account claims: "There are also many other things that Jesus did, but if these were to be described individually, I do not think the whole world would contain the books that would be written" (John 21:25).

What was retained in this stage of the Gospel tradition was crucial: stories such as Jesus touching a leper and healing him; Jesus calling his disciples and empowering them to share in his mission; Jesus embracing the children and reaching out to sinners and outcasts; Jesus calling Zacchaeus, the tax collector, down from his perch in the sycamore tree and dining with him; Jesus interpreting the Law with compassion; Jesus teaching the disciples that they had to lose their life in order to save it; Jesus celebrating a final Passover meal with his disciples; Jesus praying with anguish in the Garden of Gethsemane; Jesus dying on a cross; the Risen Jesus still bearing his wounds and bringing peace to his frightened disciples.

These stories of Jesus' life circulating orally among the various Christian communities were heard and explained and discussed. It is possible, however, that already in this second stage of the Gospel tradition some portions of the accounts about Jesus had been put in writing. The account of Jesus' final hours, for example, seems to have taken shape prior to the composition of the Gospel accounts. It is probable that already in the Jerusalem community, devout followers of Jesus would recall the sequence of events from his arrest in Gethsemane, the hearings before the high priest and the Sanhedrin, the trial before Pilate, and his torture and execution on the Cross. Celebrated in the light of the Resurrection, these final hours of Jesus were seen as an enactment of the Paschal mystery—Jesus' triumphant and life-giving passage from death to life. The remembering of these events would take place in an atmosphere of prayer and reflection, with readings from the Old Testament such as Psalm 22 that has a strong role in the Passion narratives of Mark and Matthew's Gospels.[8] Egeria, the famous pilgrim who wrote an account of her visit to Jerusalem around AD 380, describes the Christians in Jerusalem at the time of Passover celebrating the Death and Resurrection of Jesus in just this manner: prayerfully retracing the major steps of Jesus' final hours and remembering the story of his Passion. The early solidifying of the traditions about Jesus' Passion helps explain why the Passion narratives of all four Gospels are remarkably similar. Another sequence that may have taken literary shape at this stage is the coupling in Mark, Matthew, and John of the account of Jesus multiplying

The early solidifying of the traditions about Jesus' Passion helps explain why the Passion narratives of all four Gospels are remarkably similar.

---

8   See the quotation of Psalm 22:1 "My God, my God, why have you forsaken me?" as the last words of Jesus in both Mark (15:34) and Matthew (27:46).

the loaves and walking on the water—two powerful miracles proclaiming Jesus' divine power (Mark 6:34–52; Matthew 14:13–33; John 6:1–21).

Thus the early Christians sustained the memory of Jesus at the very heart of their life of faith, such as in settings of preaching, teaching, and communal worship. As we have noted, this was not simply an exercise in historical memory for these early followers of Jesus, but an expression of their faith. Through these stories of Jesus they encountered in their own time this same Jesus, now risen and present to them in their faith experience. Thus the early Christian community—the Church—selected and shaped the stream of tradition that led to the Gospels.

3. The Early Church and the Gospels: Fixing Memory in Writing

In this final stage of formation, dating from approximately AD 70 to the end of the first century, the Gospel tradition is fixed in writing through the work of the four evangelists. The early Christian community's remembrance and understanding of Jesus that had circulated orally in the way we have described, was now captured in written form in what we know as the Gospels of Matthew, Mark, Luke, and John. This does not mean that the oral tradition about Jesus ceased. Stories about Jesus would have continued to circulate in the early Church during and after the composition of the Gospels. But the fixing of much of this tradition in writing was a major milestone in the life of the apostolic Church. Before this, the oral traditions about Jesus were diverse—ever-expanding and changing as they were proclaimed and reflected on in the various local communities. Putting the stories in writing stabilized them. As they were incorporated into the New Testament canon, these Gospel narrative texts became the authoritative way of telling the story of Jesus Christ.[9]

What triggered this significant change? Several factors may have been in play. The Gospel accounts first begin to appear around AD 70, a date seared in the minds and hearts of both Jews and

---

9   On the formation of the canon, see chapter 8, pages 100–117.

Christians because it was the year in which Roman legions besieged Jerusalem and finally destroyed the Temple, the heart of Jewish life. The Temple was also sacred to Jesus and to his Jewish Christian followers. The Acts of the Apostles reports that the Christians of Jerusalem continued to pray in the Temple on a daily basis (Acts 2:42–46). And we know that when Paul came to Jerusalem, a primary purpose of his visit was to worship in the Temple (Acts 21:26). Thus for both Jews and Jewish Christians, the

The Gospel accounts first begin to appear around AD 70, a date seared in the minds and hearts of both Jews and Christians.

destruction of the Temple was a traumatic event and both communities had to rethink and reinterpret their respective religious traditions in the light of this astounding fact. For Judaism it meant turning with renewed force to the local synagogue and the family as the institutions that ultimately sustained their Jewish heritage. For the early Jewish Christians, it meant reinterpreting the meaning of the Temple in a symbolic way—Jesus himself was viewed as the real "Temple" in which God's presence was revealed (John 2:21–22) and also the Christian community itself came to be seen as the "Temple" where God's Spirit dwelled (1 Corinthians 6:19; 1 Peter 2:5). For both communities, it meant reflecting anew on the deep biblical traditions that had affirmed that the ultimate foundation of all worship was a clean heart devoted to God.[10]

This major turning point, no doubt, was one factor prompting the early Christians to take stock and to retell the story of Jesus in a way that would bring new inspiration to his followers at a time of crisis. Scholars debate the date of Mark's Gospel, most placing it right before or just after AD 70. Many of those interpreters who are convinced that Mark's account was written in Rome believe that the

---

10 For example, Isaiah 1:10–17 severely criticizes Temple worship that is not accompanied by a righteous life. Similarly, Psalm 51:18–19 prays: "For you do not desire sacrifice or I would give it; a burnt offering you would not accept. My sacrifice, O God, is a contrite spirit; a contrite, humbled heart, O God, you will not scorn."

Emperor Nero's vicious persecution of Christians in the aftermath of the great fire in that city (AD 64) forms the backdrop for this Gospel, accounting for the Gospel's strong emphasis on the sufferings of Jesus and the impact of those sufferings on Jesus' disciples. The Gospels of Matthew, Luke, and John were all written after AD 70 and in different ways reflect this same critical time of reassessment.

Another factor in the appearance of the Gospels may have been the changing nature of the Christian community itself as it moved on through history. The earliest generation of witnesses and apostolic leaders would be fading from the scene by this point and it was important that the right understanding of Jesus and his mission be continued. The expectation of Christ's final return at the Parousia, which may have been a fervent hope for some Christians in the early decades of the Church, was now understood to be in the more distant future. The realization was setting in that Christians faced an ongoing history and needed to build appropriate structures and maintain a genuine tradition. The Pastoral Letters, which were written toward the end of the first century, address this concern for authentic teachers and sound tradition.

The Gospels challenged Christians at a crucial point in their common history to follow in the way of Jesus with new inspiration and commitment. To do this, the evangelists used the literary form of a "narrative" or story. Through narrative, we can most effectively communicate the meaning and impact of a person. To describe someone we love, we could list their qualities; a far more effective and moving way, however, is to tell compelling stories about them. The ancient world knew this, too, and there were literary works such as biographies of great personages like Alexander the Great or Apollonius of Tyana. And, of course, the Old Testament—the Scriptures of the early Church—were full of vivid stories of great people such as Moses and David. Although the Gospel writers may have instinctively drawn on this type of literature, the Gospel accounts

> The evangelists used the literary form of a "narrative" or story.

are much more vivid and lively than other examples of biographies from the ancient world. Some scholars consider the literary form of the Gospels to be unique to early Christianity. We can understand why this is so—the heart of Christian faith is not a set of beliefs and rituals but a relationship with the person of Jesus Christ. Thus narratives that capture the beauty and mystery of this person are the best expression of Christian faith and the reason why the Gospels stand at the heart of the New Testament.

CHAPTER 6

The History of the New Testament: The Writing of the Four Gospels

One of the striking features of the New Testament is that there are four Gospels and not simply one. These four portrayals of Jesus are each unique, even while evidently speaking of the one and same Jesus. Imagine commissioning four great artists to portray a compelling and beloved subject—a spouse, a child, or a parent. If all four portraits were identical on completion, there would be great disappointment. Yet if the artists were accomplished, each of the four distinctive portraits would accurately capture the spirit and truth of the subject they had painted.

That the four Gospels are distinctive portrayals of Jesus shows that the early Church was not simply interested in a historical reconstruction of Jesus' life and ministry. Instead, as we noted earlier, they wanted to proclaim the meaning of this beloved and compelling figure by drawing on traditions about Jesus rooted in history; traditions selected and shaped to make the Risen Jesus, the Jesus of faith, present for those who believed in him. The names assigned to the four Gospels in the second century (names are not included in the original Gospels themselves) express this point: the Gospel *according to* Mark, *according to* Matthew, and so on. The phrase "according to" suggests that each of the four evangelists witnesses in a unique way to the one Gospel embodied in the person of Jesus.

The distinctiveness of each Gospel was a by-product of converging factors: (1) each of the Gospels was written in a specific context and at a specific time; (2) each of the Gospels draws in different ways on traditions about Jesus available to it; and (3) each of the evangelists—the final composers of the Gospel texts—had different literary styles and capacities. Although drawing on an array of sources and traditions, the Gospels were not written by a "committee." Each account reveals a particular and consistent Greek style, evidence of a single final author, even if, as in the case of John's Gospel, it may have gone through more than one edition before its final composition.

The Gospel according to Mark

Virtually all modern biblical scholars agree that the Gospel of Mark was the first to be written, sometime right before or shortly after AD 70. Scholars debate where the Gospel may have originated. The historian Eusebius (AD 260–340) records that Papias, a bishop from Hierapolis in Asia Minor, testified around AD 90 that Mark's Gospel originated in Rome and that Mark was a kind of secretary for the Apostle Peter, the source of Mark's information about Jesus. We cannot be sure how reliable Papias' testimony is, but there is evidence in Mark that makes a Roman context for his Gospel plausible, particularly the impact of Nero's persecution of the Church there. Other scholars prefer a Palestinian setting for Mark, with the evangelist writing right before or shortly after the cataclysm of the Jewish revolt against Rome and the violent ending of that revolt in AD 70. Both settings would explain Mark's strong emphasis on the Passion of Jesus and the struggles of his disciples in the face of suffering and death.

A recent trend in scholarship has emphasized that the Gospels were written in and to a local church context. Mark, for example, would be viewed as writing for his Christian community, probably in Rome, battered by persecution and seeking to find healing and inspiration. Others, however, have challenged this view and suggested that the evangelists wrote their Gospels "for all Christians" and not just for their own local community.[1] A strong network of communication connected early Christian communities throughout the Mediterranean world. Paul's letters seem to have circulated rather rapidly beyond the particular communities he addressed. The First Letter of Peter is addressed to several communities in north and central Asia Minor (1 Peter 1:1), clearly indicating that there were some contacts among these Christian groups. Mark may have written his Gospel in concert with and to a particular community, such as the Christian community of Rome, but with the realization that his work might, if received well, be circulated to other communities. Thus the Gospels were both local and global at the same time.

> Paul's letters seem to have circulated rather rapidly beyond the particular communities he addressed.

If, in fact, Mark is the first Gospel to be written, then it is to this evangelist we owe the remarkably creative act of presenting the life of Jesus in narrative form, an act that would set the pace for the rest of the four Gospels. The evangelist, of course, was not working in isolation but lived and worked within a living stream of tradition and understanding about Jesus, a tradition shaped by the mature faith of the Christian community itself.

Mark gives a fundamental literary structure to his narrative by dividing it into three parts that take place in three geographical areas: the bulk of Jesus' ministry of teaching and healing in the northern region of Galilee, then the fateful journey of Jesus and his disciples from Galilee to Jerusalem, and finally in Jerusalem a last confrontation with his opponents and the climactic events of Jesus' Passion and Death. Mark also proclaims the Resurrection of Jesus—the heart of Christian faith—but does so with a certain indirection. In Mark's account the male disciples flee at the moment of the arrest, with Peter trailing along to the High Priest's house, only to deny

---

1   The phrase is from a book edited by Richard Bauckham, *The Gospels for All Christians: Rethinking the Gospel Audiences* (Grand Rapids: Eerdmans, 1998).

Jesus at the very moment Jesus himself is fearlessly confronting his opponents. Yet the women who witness the Crucifixion of Jesus discover the empty tomb and hear the announcement of the heavenly messenger that Jesus, who was crucified, was not to be found in the tomb: "He has been raised; he is not here" (Mark 16:6). These same women are told to announce this astounding reality to his disciples and to instruct them to go to Galilee where they will see him "as he told you" (16:7).

Mark's blunt, forceful, and relatively spare narrative would set the pattern for both Matthew and Luke's Gospels.

The Gospel according to Matthew

This narrative draws heavily on Mark's Gospel as its primary source. Some 600 of the 660 verses of Mark's Gospel find their way into Matthew's account, and the overall pattern of Mark's story, moving from Galilee to Jerusalem, remains intact. Yet Matthew's Gospel is distinctly different from Mark's. Matthew includes a lot of material not found in Mark, particularly an abundance of the sayings of Jesus; sayings that may have been gathered into a collection of Jesus' teachings prior to Matthew's Gospel.[2] Matthew shapes this teaching material into five great discourses that appear in the course of Jesus' ministry, such as the Sermon on the Mount (chapters 5–7), the mission discourse (chapter 10), the parable discourse (chapter 13), the community discourse (chapter 18), and the apocalyptic discourse (chapters 24–25). Matthew also draws on traditions that seem to be unique to his community, such as the stories surrounding Jesus' conception and infancy (chapters 1–2), the strong condemnation of the Pharisees (chapter 23), and the final appearance of the Risen Christ to his disciples on a mountaintop in Galilee when he commissions them to bring the Gospel to "all nations" (28:16–20).

---

2   Scholars refer to this hypothetical source as "Q" from the German word *Quelle* or "source." No independent copies of Q exist; it is detectable only in the common material found in Matthew and Luke but not in Mark.

Equally important is the overall Jewish tone that characterizes Matthew's Gospel. Matthew draws heavily on the Old Testament, with quotations from the Scriptures marking virtually all the aspects of Jesus' life. He also portrays Jesus profoundly respecting the Jewish Law and declaring at the outset of his ministry: "Do not think that I have come to abolish the law or the prophets. I have come not to abolish but to fulfill" (Matthew 5:17). The Jesus of Matthew's Gospel does not disregard the Law but interprets it with compassion in accordance with the love command (22:34–40), an interpretation that Matthew's Jewish Christian community would consider compelling for them. In Matthew's narrative, too, the mission of Jesus is centered on his people Israel (10:5–6; 15:24); only after the Resurrection does the Risen Christ send his disciples to "all nations" (28:19), the ultimate intent of God's love for the world.

Why did Matthew's Gospel account have these characteristics, and why would the evangelist and his community decide to produce another Gospel beyond that of Mark, which they must have known and revered? The answer may be found in the context in which Matthew's Gospel was composed. Most interpreters of Matthew, drawing on evidence within the Gospel itself, believe that the evangelist wrote this Gospel for a Jewish Christian community that found itself in a period of wrenching transition. As noted earlier, the destruction of the Jerusalem Temple in AD 70 triggered profound transitions for both Judaism and Jewish Christianity.

> Matthew wrote this Gospel for a Jewish Christian community that found itself in a period of wrenching transition.

It was also a time of growing tension for the leaders of Judaism, who were, in a sense, having to "rebuild" their Jewish heritage in a radically different context—with no Temple, no priesthood, and with the ever increasing intrusion of Roman might. They were aiming for consolidation and unity, and thus were less tolerant of fringe groups, among whom were the Jewish followers of Jesus.

At the same time, the Jewish Christians themselves were at a crossroads. On the one hand, they had to affirm the authenticity of their "Jewishness" in the face of criticism from their fellow Jews that they were abandoning or betraying their Jewish heritage. (We can think of Paul's sharp opposition to the Christian movement even before the calamity of AD 70). On the other hand, they were also facing the fact that increasing numbers of Gentiles were joining the community and some feared that the sacred traditions of their ancestors would be lost or diluted. It is likely that Matthew's Gospel was written precisely to address these "two fronts" by reassuring his fellow Jewish Christians that in following Jesus the Messiah they were not abandoning their Jewish heritage but in fact were experiencing its "fullness," while reminding his community that obedience to God's will required that the community be open to welcoming Gentiles into their midst, a fulfillment of the command of the Risen Christ.

Many interpreters of Matthew's Gospel believe that it was composed in the city of Antioch. The third largest city of the Roman Empire, Antioch was strategically located on the trade routes from east to west. It had a significant Jewish population along with its majority of Gentiles. And we recall from our discussion of Paul that early in Antioch there was an important Christian community composed of both Jewish Christians and Gentile Christians. It was here, the Acts of the Apostles notes, that the followers of Jesus were first called "Christians" (Acts 11:26) and here, too, we know from both the testimony of Paul and the Acts of the Apostles, that there were some tensions about the inclusion of Gentiles within the still predominately Jewish Christian community (Acts 11:19–26; Galatians 2:11–14). And finally, it was in the post-New Testament church of Antioch that the earliest citation of Matthew's Gospel is found.

This Antioch setting suggests a possible scenario for why and how Matthew composed his Gospel. Given the strong Jewish accent of Matthew's Gospel, it is likely that the community from which this Gospel ultimately came had originated in Palestine itself, perhaps in the northern region of Galilee. It is there that the community may have had access to the collections of Jesus' sayings (the Q source) and some of the other traditions special to Matthew, such as the material about Jesus' genealogy, conception, and early years—all of which have a strong Jewish and Old Testament flavor. The chaos of the Jewish uprising against Rome and the destruction of the Jerusalem Temple may have prompted Matthew's community to move north to Syria and ultimately to Antioch. There his community would have come in contact with Mark's Gospel, with its strong emphasis on the miracles of Jesus and the account of his Passion and Death. Armed with additional material about Jesus not found in Mark's Gospel, and faced with a different context in the transition facing his Jewish Christian community, Matthew apparently chose to expand and rewrite the Gospel account provided by Mark. This was done not because Mark's Gospel was dishonored but because the evolving circumstance of the Christian community called for a new form of witness. Although tradition credits the Gospel to the Apostle Matthew, we cannot be sure that the original follower of Jesus composed this text. It could be, however, that a community associated with Matthew stands at the origin of this Gospel.

And so the Gospel of Matthew would be born. Because of its rich portrayal of Jesus as teacher and healer, it circulated widely in the early Church and served as something of a "catechetical" resource for Christian communities beyond that of Antioch, the mother church of the Pauline mission.

The Gospel according to Luke and the Acts of the Apostles

Like the Gospel of Matthew, but independently of it, the account of Luke used both the Gospel of Mark and a collection of Jesus' teachings as primary sources, along with special materials available to Luke but not found in the other Gospels. Luke crafts a Gospel that is unique, not only in its own distinctive portrayal of the life of Jesus but also because he fuses on to his Gospel narrative a second volume, the Acts of the Apostles, an account of the spread of the Gospel from Jerusalem to Rome, and to "the ends of the earth" (Acts 1:8).

As we have already noted, Luke is the one evangelist who begins his Gospel with a formal preface, addressed to "most excellent Theophilus" (Luke 1:1–4). Theophilus may have been an actual person—perhaps the benefactor supporting Luke's work—or a kind of ideal but symbolic reader (the name "Theophilus" means "beloved by God" in Greek). Luke tells Theophilus that he wants to write down "in an orderly sequence" the "events that have been fulfilled among us." The purpose is to help his reader "realize the certainty of the teachings you have received." The word "certainty" (*asphaleian* in Greek) used by Luke here means more than simply historical accuracy but a sense of "reliability" or "trustworthiness." In other words, Luke wants to show that the whole string of events from the life of Jesus through to the spread of the Gospel into the whole world was not by chance but part of God's providential plan of salvation.

That plan, Luke's narrative emphasizes, has its roots in the people Israel. Luke begins his narrative in the Jerusalem Temple with a host of deeply pious and faithful Jews: the priest Zachary and his wife Elizabeth; Anna and Simeon, two devout Jews who virtually live in the Temple and who will welcome the infant Jesus to his Father's house; and, of course, Mary and Joseph. The boy Jesus himself loves the Temple and remains behind when his family begins the journey home from their pilgrimage to Jerusalem: "Did you not know that I must be in my Father's house?" (Luke 2:49).

Jerusalem will continue to play a major role in Luke's account, as Jesus is "resolutely determined to journey to Jerusalem" (9:51) in the course of his ministry. Luke draws the idea of Jesus' journey from his source Mark, but expands the notion in his own Gospel.

Luke draws the idea of Jesus' journey from his source Mark, but expands the notion in his own Gospel.

When Jesus comes over the crest of the Mount of Olives and sees the city and its glorious Temple laid out before him, he weeps out of love for this city and because of sadness at its impending doom (Luke 19:41). It is in Jerusalem that Jesus will face his Passion and Crucifixion, as well as the triumph of his Resurrection. Unlike Mark's and Matthew's accounts in which the Risen Christ appears to his disciples in Galilee, Luke confines the appearances of the Risen Christ to Jerusalem itself, including the beautiful story unique to Luke of Jesus' encounter with the disciples on the way to Emmaus. After Jesus has explained the Scriptures and as he is breaking bread with them, these disciples recognize the Risen Christ and, with their hearts burning within them, return to Jerusalem to join the other disciples (Luke 24:13–35).

The Jerusalem setting and the events that take place there following the Resurrection prepare the reader for Luke's second volume, the Acts of the Apostles. Luke alone narrates the Ascension—the culmination of Jesus' ministry (Luke 24:50–53). The Risen Christ is now exalted to the right hand of God and sends down on his frail disciples the gift of the Spirit, events Luke tells in the opening chapters of Acts (2:1–13). The power of the Spirit will drive the community out beyond the closed doors of the upper room into the world to be Christ's "witnesses." The words of the Risen Christ set forth the overall structure of the Acts of the Apostles: "But you will receive power when the holy Spirit comes upon you, and you will be my witnesses in Jerusalem, throughout Judea and Samaria, and to the ends of the earth" (Acts 1:8).

The first several chapters of Acts concentrate on the life and mission of the Jerusalem community, led by Peter and the Apostles. Paul, the future Apostle to the Gentiles, makes his appearance in chapter 9 with his dramatic conversion on the road to Damascus. After the council in Jerusalem (Acts 15), which endorses the Gentile mission already undertaken by Paul, Barnabas, and others, it is Paul's missionary journeys that command the attention of the remainder of Acts. The finale comes when Paul, under arrest in Caesarea Maritima, is taken by ship as a prisoner to Rome, where he will be under house arrest. The tumultuous journey of Paul through storm and shipwreck ends with the Apostle continuing to preach the Gospel from his imprisonment. The final line of Acts both concludes the story and projects it into the future: "And with complete assurance and without hindrance [Paul] proclaimed the kingdom of God and taught about the Lord Jesus Christ" (Acts 28:31).

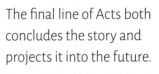

The final line of Acts both concludes the story and projects it into the future.

Luke's overall portrayal of the "events that have been fulfilled among us" in his Gospel and in Acts moves in a dramatic sweep of history. God's plan of salvation begins with the people Israel, flowers in the ministry of Jesus, and, through the power of the Spirit, spreads throughout the world through the witness and proclamation of the disciples of Jesus.

Luke's narrative style is vivid and memorable. Some of the most beloved stories about Jesus in the New Testament come from Luke's hand: the endearing and joyous stories of Jesus' birth celebrated every year at the Christmas season (in contrast to Matthew's infancy narrative that is much more sober in tone); the parables such as the prodigal son, the good Samaritan, the rich man and Lazarus, the Pharisee and the publican; or incidents found only in Luke such as Jesus' calling of Peter and his first disciples in a boat on the Sea of Galilee (5:1–11), or the poignant account of the woman who washes Jesus' feet with her hair in the house of Simon the Pharisee (7:36–50), or his fierce words about Herod (13:31–33); or his encounter with Zacchaeus in his sycamore tree (19:1–10). The same is true of the many events found in the Acts of the Apostles, from the dramatic experience of Pentecost to the gripping account of Paul's final sea journey.

While we can surmise that Luke, similar to Matthew, used the Gospel of Mark and a collection of Jesus' sayings as primary sources for his Gospel account, the sources for the Acts of the Apostles are much harder to determine. Some scholars question the historical reliability of much of the material in Acts, suggesting that the evangelist crafted this account from his knowledge of Paul's letters, from Old Testament reflections, and from his own creative imagination.

But most scholars give Luke's account much more historical credit. As we have noted above, Luke had a theological or pastoral purpose in crafting his Gospel and the Acts of the Apostles. It is evident that Luke emphasizes continuity in the life of the early Church in a way that may have smoothed over some of the bumps and discontinuities of the actual history. Likewise, Luke may have composed some of the speeches found in Acts such as that of Peter (3:12–26), or Stephen (7:1–53). But

> Luke had a theological or pastoral purpose in crafting his Gospel and the Acts of the Apostles.

the overall account that Luke gives us regarding the events and spirit of the Jerusalem church and the spread of the Christian mission to the west through the ministry of Paul and his coworkers surely drew on historical sources.

One possible source for some of the material is the experience of the author himself. In such passages as Acts 16:10–17; 20:5–15; 21:1–18; 27:1—28:16, the narrator uses "we" implying that at these points in the narrative the author (or a source he is using) was a companion of Paul. We should also note the remarkable cast of characters and the many events and locations that are named in the Acts of the Apostles. The overall description of the landscape and the unfolding events of the early Church—including, we should note, some of its problems and disputes such as the struggles between Paul and John Mark (Acts 15:36–41) or the tension between the Hebrew-speaking and Greek-speaking Jewish Christians in the Jerusalem church (Acts 6:1–7)—are compatible with what we know of first-century history. Similar to the Gospels themselves, Acts draws on historical sources while pursuing its primary goal of using this historical backdrop to proclaim the Gospel of Jesus Christ.

Who was Luke the Evangelist? And when and where did he write his Gospel and the Acts of the Apostles? As with the other Gospsels, there are no certain answers. The name "Luke" was assigned to the Gospel by a later second-century tradition. Some have noted that Paul refers to a Luke in Philemon 24 as one of his "co-workers." In the concluding section of 2 Timothy, the author (Paul?) laments that "Luke is the only one with me" (4:11). Paul also refers to Luke in Colossians 4:14 as "the beloved physician"—a reference that prompted a still-surviving tradition that the evangelist was a doctor. Some have even found echoes of this in the evangelist's compassionate stories of Jesus' healings in the Gospel. We cannot be certain that any of these references to "Luke" is the Evangelist Luke, but it is not improbable.

Some scholars also speculate that Luke was a resident of Antioch, a tradition still strong in that region today. This would help associate Luke with Paul and his missionary journeys. A slender thread of evidence for Luke's presence in Antioch is the supposition that the evangelist Luke is the same as the "Lucius" mentioned among members of the church in Antioch in Acts 13:1 and in Paul's list of coworkers who send greetings from Corinth in Romans 16:21.

Whoever the actual author of these two New Testament books may have been, he was writing to give perspective to Gentile Christians about the origin, spirit, and powerful dynamic reality of their Christian faith. Some scholars believe that along with this theological purpose, Luke wanted to also reassure Roman imperial authorities that they had nothing to fear from the Christian movement, despite the false accusations of its opponents. In Acts, Peter, Paul, and other early Christian missionaries are harassed and imprisoned, but Luke shows that this was because of false testimony against them. He demonstrates their innocence and loyalty through the respect they show representatives of the Empire, as in Paul's respectful responses to the procurators Felix and Festus (Acts, chapters 24–26), or the way Paul and his companions rescue their jailor from suicide in Philippi (Acts 16:25–40). Christians could be good citizens and were not trying to overthrow the Empire.

Other scholarship, however, has offered a more convincing interpretation of Luke's perspective. While it is true that on one level the Acts of the Apostles does not portray the Christians as revolutionaries, on a deeper level it portrays Christianity as deeply subversive to the values and authority of the Roman Empire. Jesus himself is the exalted king over all kings, including the emperor. The way of life early Christians led in his name—a communal life that exemplified love, respect, mutual sharing of goods, selfless service, and complete devotion to God above all other authority—was a vision of human life that ran radically counter to imperial ideology.

Acts portrays Christianity as deeply subversive to the values and authority of the Roman Empire. Jesus himself is the exalted king over all kings, including the emperor.

We do not know for sure where and to whom Luke composed his two-volume work. It is possible that there was a span of time between his writing of the Gospel and the Acts, although both the evident continuity and the parallels between the two works make more sense if they were written at the same time. We also do not know the precise location from which Luke wrote. Many suggest Ephesus, a major Gentile city and one where Paul spent considerable time. We do know that the author of Luke and Acts, writing sometime in the last quarter of the first century to a Gentile audience immersed within the life of the Roman Empire, offered the Church a powerful portrayal of Jesus and the dynamic mission that would be carried out in his name.

The Gospel according to John

Of all four Gospel accounts, the Gospel of John is the most distinctive. One modern commentator has branded John as the "Maverick Gospel," an apt description.[3] Even a quick comparison of John and the synoptic Gospels reveals a number of clear differences: in John's account, Jesus chooses his first disciples from among the disciples of John the Baptist near the river Jordan (John 1:35–42), unlike the synoptics where Jesus first chooses Galilean fishermen. John begins the

---

3   See the work of Robert Kysar, *John, the Maverick Gospel* (Louisville: Westminster/John Knox Press, rev. ed., 1996).

public ministry of Jesus at the wedding feast of Cana in Galilee (John 2:1–12), followed immediately by Jesus going to Jerusalem and his dramatic prophetic action in the Temple (2:13–22), an event that comes at the end of Jesus' ministry in the other Gospels. The synoptic Gospels portray Jesus taking only one dramatic journey to Jerusalem during his ministry, but John has Jesus moving back and forth to Jerusalem several times. The keynote of Jesus' ministry in the synoptic Gospels—announcing the coming "Kingdom of God"—is hardly mentioned in John. There are no exorcisms in John's account, nor any parables—all characteristic of Jesus' ministry in the synoptics. Finally, the Johannine Jesus speaks in long, meditative discourses, unlike the more proverbial-type sayings in the synoptics.

Whereas Peter is the prominent spokesperson for the disciples in the synoptic Gospels, that role later in John's Gospel seems to be taken over by the "Beloved Disciple"—an unnamed disciple who has special access to Jesus at the Last Supper (13:23–25). This person enables Peter to witness Jesus' trial (18:15), and he is present at the Cross (while Peter has left the scene in disgrace). Jesus declares the Beloved Disciple to be the son of his mother and, at the same time, entrusts his mother to this disciple's care (19:26–27). His testimony underscores the meaning of Jesus' Death (19:35), he runs to the empty tomb with Peter (and waits for Peter to catch up), and he "believes" while Peter remains confused (20:8).

The two disciples also appear in chapter 21, which seems to be something of an appendix to John's account. There in this exquisite scene at the breakfast prepared by the Risen Christ on the seashore, Jesus draws from the repentant Peter a threefold expression of

> Clearly in John, while respecting the traditional role of Peter, the author shows the Beloved Disciple to be favored by Jesus.

love, restoring him to his discipleship. Subsequently Peter asks Jesus about the fate of the "Beloved Disciple" and Jesus replies: "What if I want him to remain until I come?" (21:23). Clearly in John, while respecting the traditional role of Peter, the author shows the Beloved

Disciple to be favored by Jesus and he is the one whose testimony apparently underwrites the authenticity of the Gospel's own portrayal of Jesus: "It is this disciple who testifies to these things and has written them, and we know that his testimony is true" (21:24).

This list of differences could go on but the point is clear: while the focus of all four Gospels is on the person of Jesus and his mission, John's portrayal is unique. John emphasizes from the outset of his Gospel that Jesus is the "Word [that] became flesh" (1:14), the Word sent by God to reveal God's unquenchable love for the world—a love embodied and manifested in the person and mission of Jesus himself. Thus the miracles of Jesus become in John "signs" of that love; his words, an expression of that redeeming love; and, above all, the Death of Jesus, which John interprets as an act of one who lays down his life for his friends (15:13), is the most complete expression of Jesus' mission to reveal God's love to the world.

Why is John's Gospel so different? Some years ago many Johannine scholars attributed John's unique qualities to the fact that this Gospel was written later than the other three and was thoroughly influenced by Greco-Roman culture. The transcendent language of John's Gospel and its meditative discourses seemed similar to non-Christian literature of the late first and second centuries. In addition, John's Gospel was discounted for not having any information about the actual historical setting of Jesus' lifetime. John's portrayal of Jesus seemed to be in line with the initial phases of gnostic Christianity that downplayed the humanity of Jesus.

Some of the Dead Sea documents have a style of discourse similar to that of John.

The discovery of the Dead Sea scrolls and their portrayal of a Jewish movement contemporary with the life of Jesus and the early Church changed this prevailing view of John in a dramatic way. Some of the Dead Sea documents have a style of discourse similar to that of John. They use similar symbolic language and, like John's account, consider good and evil to be clear-cut opposites that never overlap (a position called dualism). The Dead Sea scrolls, along with other modern archaeological discoveries, have given us a more nuanced view of Jewish life and thought at the time of Jesus. It was much more diverse than earlier generations of scholars had assumed.

Scholars began to see that John's Gospel fits with perspectives and literary styles that existed in Palestinian Judaism of the first century. They also noted that while John's literary style might appear to be more abstract and transcendent than that of the synoptics, in many ways that Gospel has its feet firmly planted in first century Judaism. John is well aware of the topography of Jerusalem and its Temple—more so than the synoptics themselves. Thus, for example, he identifies the Sheep Gate and the pools of Bethesda (John 5:2), and the pool of Siloam (9:7), details not referred to in the synoptics and realities confirmed by modern archaeology many centuries later. John also implies that Roman soldiers accompanied the Temple guards to arrest Jesus in Gethsemane, a probability in the circumstances of Jerusalem at the time (18:3). John names Annas as the father-in-law of Caiphas, another intriguing historical detail (18:13), and he is also aware of the feasts of Judaism—Sukkoth or "Tabernacles" (7:2), Hanukkah, "the Feast of the Dedication" (10:22), and, of course, Passover (13:1). He also makes subtle use of Old Testament symbols throughout his Gospel. For example, in John, the three Passion predictions mentioned in the synoptic Gospels are transformed into Jesus' sayings about being "lifted up"—both on the Cross and in exaltation, a type of double meaning favored by John (see 3:14). John tells us that he takes the symbol from the strange incident narrated in Numbers 21:9, where Moses lifts up the bronze serpent in order to heal the Israelites after their sin of rebellion.

The Evolution of the Johannine Community

A number of scholars have proposed a possible scenario that led to the formation of John's Gospel, drawing on hints within the Gospel itself.[4] For example, the community that ultimately produced this Gospel may have originated in what we might call "heterodox" Judaism. John indicates that Jesus recruited his first disciples from among the disciples of John the Baptist, a reform movement not unlike the Essenes who also went to the desert to symbolize a renewed beginning for Israel in reaction to what they saw as the deadly compromises of the Hasmonean dynasty.[5] The Jews who followed the Baptist would already have had a different perspective from other more establishment type Jews.

A second step may have been the influx of Samaritan Jews into this maverick community. Early in John's Gospel, Jesus goes to Samaria and there meets the woman at the well, one of the most famous stories in John's account. After their enticing conversation, the woman goes and announces that she has met "a man who told me everything I have done. Could he possibly be the Messiah?" (4:29). Her testimony convinces the other Samaritans and they go out to see Jesus and invite him to stay with them. The story concludes with the townspeople acknowledging their faith in Jesus as "the savior of the world" (4:42). This mission of Jesus to the Samaritans is not mentioned in the other Gospels, although the Acts of the Apostles reports Philip's successful preaching of the Gospel to them as well (see Acts 8:4–8). The Samaritans were considered outcasts by the majority of Jews, and Samaritans had little respect for Jerusalem and its Davidic traditions. Their preferred place of worship was Mount Gerizim, as the Samaritan woman reminds Jesus (John 4:20). If a significant number of Samaritan Jews were part of the Johannine community, this might help explain why the motif of the "Kingdom of God,"

> This mission of Jesus to the Samaritans is not mentioned in the other Gospels.

---

4   See, for example, Raymond E. Brown's *The Community of the Beloved Disciple: The Life, Loves, and Hates of an Individual Church in New Testament Times* (New York: Paulist, 1979).

5   See pages 29–30.

which drew on God's promise for an unending Davidic kingdom, would not be a favored concept in the Gospel of John.

Another stage would be the growing tension between the early Jewish Christian community and the religious leaders of the dominant majority, as we saw in the case of Matthew's community.[6] That tension brewing especially within the difficult post–AD 70 period for both communities may be reflected in the sharp opposition between the religious leaders and Jesus throughout John's Gospel. Unfortunately, John's Gospel tends to lump all of the leaders under the term "the Jews," which in later Christian history would stoke anti-Jewish bias on the part of many Christians and their leaders.[7] For John's community, itself Jewish in origin and character, this could not have been meant in a spirit of anti-Semitism; in later centuries, however, Christians would have become unaware of the original meaning intended by John. The story of the man born blind in chapter 9 of John's Gospel seems to reflect this growing tension and hostility. The parents of the man are afraid to explain to the religious leaders how their son was cured of his blindness: "His parents said this because they were afraid of the Jews, for the Jews had already agreed that if anyone acknowledged him as the Messiah, he would be expelled from the synagogue" (John 9:22).

A final stage may have come with the actual movement of the Johannine community out of Palestine into the Greco-Roman world, perhaps to Ephesus where there was later a strong tradition of John's presence. We see hints of this in the Gospel when Jesus' opponents take his words about going away to a place where they cannot find him to mean that he was going to the diaspora: "Where is he going that we will not find him? Surely he is not going to the dispersion among the Greeks to teach the Greeks, is he?" (7:35). Later in the Gospel, shortly before the Passion of Jesus, some Greeks who had come to Jerusalem for the feast of Passover approach the disciples,

---

6 See pages 75–78.

7 On this issue, see the title edited by R. Bieringer, D. Pollefeyt, and F. Vandecasteele-Vanneuville, *Anti-Judaism and the Fourth Gospel* (Assen: Royal Van Gorcum, 2001).

asking to see Jesus (12:20–21). When their request is presented to Jesus, it seems to trigger in him an awareness of his impending Death (12:23–33).

Thus the Johannine community may have been deeply rooted in Palestinian Judaism, yet shaped by some outlying groups within the orbit of early first-century Judaism—accounting for some of its distinctive theology and literary style. Later friction with the dominant majority of Jews may also be reflected in the sharp hostility between Jesus and the religious leaders in John's Gospel. And in the course of its history, the community may have physically moved to a new location, away from the chaos of post–70 Roman Palestine, and to a place such as the major city of Ephesus. That would account for some of the Hellenistic traits of this Gospel. This scenario—which is a hypothesis but not an unreasonable one—would place the final composition of John's Gospel late in the first century.

Postscript: The Johannine Letters

We should note here that some interpreters consider the three Johannine letters, also among the New Testament books, as a "final stage" in the development of the Johannine community. The three letters are each different in format, and the First Letter of John is really not a letter at all, as it has no greeting or any of the standard traits of a letter. It is better identified as a "treatise" or exhortation from the author urging his community to remain faithful to the "word of life" proclaimed by Jesus and to hold firm to the love command that was the heart of his teaching. It is this first letter that accords most closely with the Gospel of John.

The second and third letters are indeed letters but each is very brief and each is distinctive in turn. The Second Letter of John comes from the "Presbyter" (in Greek, the "Elder") who writes to warn his community (named metaphorically "the chosen lady" and "her children whom I love in truth") to hold fast to the love command and to resist the influence of "deceivers" who are bringing false doctrines into the community (2 John 7–11). The Third Letter of John addresses an individual, "Gaius," and complains about "Diotrephes" who does not acknowledge the authority of the Elder and is a cause of division in the community.

A probable scenario for these letters, suggested by many scholars, is that they were written sometime after the Gospel of John, therefore near the end of the first century or at the beginning of the second, and that the underlying problems addressed have to do with a division brewing in the Johannine community. It could be that the transcendent qualities of John's portrayal of Jesus were being misinterpreted by early gnostic or docetist groups who tended to discount the humanity of Jesus. Thus the final stage of the Johannine community described above would be a split, with some groups moving to the fringe of the Christian community and the majority remaining faithful to the Gospel and retaining their bonds with the rest of the early Church.

Relation of John's Gospel to the Synoptics

The later dating of John's Gospel raises the question of John's relationship to the synoptic Gospels, a topic that continues to be debated. Was the evangelist who produced John's Gospel familiar with the other Gospels and yet decided, in the context of his unique community, to write such a different portrayal of Jesus and his mission? Or did the evangelist have no acquaintance with the synoptic Gospels? In this case, John's Gospel would represent an independent stream of tradition parallel to but independent of the type of traditions about Jesus that shaped the synoptic Gospels. Others have proposed something of a middle ground solution. Evidence of parallels between some materials in John and the synoptics, such as the combination of the stories of the multiplication of the loaves and Jesus' walking on the water, as well as the close sequence in all four Passion narratives, suggests that, while John and the synoptics represent two different streams of tradition in the early Church, these traditions at some point may have had contact with each other. Some of the stories about Jesus would have circulated both in the communities that produced the Gospels of Mark, Matthew, and Luke, as well as in the community that ultimately produced John's Gospel.

In any case, John's Gospel is a profound portrayal of Jesus—the Word made flesh. The overall vision of the Gospel is first articulated in its prologue (1:1–18) in which the Word is sent from God into the world and becomes "flesh." That Word is carried out in the discourses and signs of Jesus' public ministry, and comes to its climax with the life-giving Death of Jesus that fully expresses God's redeeming love for the world and leads to Jesus' triumphant return to his father, thereby revealing the destiny of all who believe in Jesus Christ and who will share in this same bond of love between Father and Son.

When all is said and done, we do not know who the author of this Gospel is. Tradition identifies the unnamed "Beloved Disciple" mentioned in the Gospel as the Apostle John. This ancient tradition cannot be ruled out, but we also cannot guarantee its historical accuracy. In any case, this "maverick community" has given Christianity a lasting treasure.

Conclusion: The Fourfold Witness to the Risen Christ That Grounds Our Faith

The journey from the life and times of Jesus himself to the writing of the four Gospels forms a complex and rich history. The compelling witness of all four Gospels about the identity of Jesus as the Risen Christ and the character of his teaching and example, stands at the very foundation of our Christian faith. Already in the New Testament we see that the four rich expressions of the Gospel call for a Church that is not only bound in the unity of faith, but also welcomes diversity of culture and perspective. Having tracked the history of how the Bible was formed, both Old and New Testaments, we now need to view the Scriptures from the explicit vantage point of faith—the only vantage point that gives the Scriptures their true meaning.

CHAPTER 7

The Bible as the Word of God

When the reader concludes the first Scripture reading at the Eucharist, he or she says, "The Word of the Lord" and the congregation replies, "Thanks be to God." Similarly, when the priest or deacon finishes reading the Gospel for that day, he acclaims, "The Gospel of Lord," and the congregation responds, "Praise to you, Lord Jesus Christ." Those responses, along with all the other marks of reverence that surround the reading of the Scriptures at the Eucharist, make clear that the Bible readings are no ordinary literature. For people of faith, the Scriptures are in fact the "Word of God."

A Consistent Theology of the Word

Since the Second Vatican Council the Church has engaged in a strong and consistent reflection on what we mean by the "Word of God" as the underlying reality of the Scriptures. The explanation found in the Council's *Dogmatic Constitution on Divine Revelation*, known as *Dei Verbum*, is groundbreaking.[1] This statement on Divine Revelation was echoed in subsequent Church documents.[2] More importantly, its theology of the "Word of God" lays out, from a Catholic point of view, the theological foundation for understanding the nature of the Bible as truly "God's Word." One can trace five cascading phases in the revelation of God's Word that ultimately inform the whole of Scripture:

---

1   For a thorough analysis of the formation and content of this key document, see Ronald D. Witherup's *Scripture Dei Verbum (Rediscovering Vatican II)*; (New York: Paulist Press, 2006), 1–31.

2   In particular, Pope Benedict XVI's *The Word of the Lord (Verbum Domini)*, paragraph 3, who explicitly links his reflections on the Word to *Dei Verbum*. Likewise, the recent statement of the Pontifical Biblical Commission, *The Inspiration and Truth of Sacred Scripture* (Collegeville: Liturgical Press, 2014) begins by noting the foundational work of *Dei Verbum* and *Verbum Domini*; see pages 1–2.

1. First and foremost, *Dei Verbum* roots the ultimate origin of the Word of God within the Trinity itself. The God revealed in the Bible and proclaimed in Christian tradition is a God who wishes to reveal himself to the world. In the mystery of the Trinity we affirm that the one true God is also totally relational—the very nature of God defined in an eternal dynamic of mutual love among Father, Son, and Spirit. It is from this very life of God that the divine impulse to create and to be in relationship with the world springs. This is evident in the account of creation that begins the biblical saga in Genesis chapter 1. Through his all-powerful Word, God creates the universe in all of its dimensions and in all of its beauty. Above all, God creates the human being, male and female, as the summit of creation and establishes a loving relationship with humans.

2. The Bible portrays the human person, male and female, as made in the divine image: "Then God said: 'Let us make human beings in our image, after our likeness'" (Genesis 1:26); therefore as capable, indeed destined, to respond to God. Thus revelation at its root is a relationship between God and the world he created. Made in the image of God, the human person has both the capacity and the destiny to respond to God, to be in relationship and communion with God. This is fundamental to the whole theology of the Word developed in *Dei Verbum* and continuing to the present day. Official summations or creedal statements of our beliefs that flow from this relationship with God are, of course, both legitimate and necessary in order for the Church to be faithful to its own heritage over the centuries. But, at its heart, revelation is not a set of theological propositions, however important, but a loving relationship that God offers to his creatures.

3. The God who creates the universe does not stay aloof from his creation, but is involved, although mysteriously, in human history. The long and tortured saga of Israel presented in the Bible reflects this conviction. God is present—protecting Israel, admonishing it, forgiving it, carrying it forward, often in spite of itself. Although, as we have seen, the main focus of the Bible is on God's unique people

Israel and its complex history, the God of Israel is also the God of the nations and the entire history of all peoples and of the universe itself is God's arena.

4. The culmination of human history and of the revealing Word of God comes in the person of Jesus Christ, the Word made flesh and the definitive revealer of God's Word to the world. Here *Dei Verbum*, as does Pope Benedict's *Verbum Domini*, turns to the prologue of John's Gospel for the characteristic biblical illustration of this conviction (John 1:1–18). The Word who is with God from the beginning is the Word spoken by God and perfectly expressing God's being so that the Word *is* God (John 1:1). This is the Word that John's poetic prologue describes as arcing from the very bosom of God into the created world and becoming flesh. In the flesh of Jesus Christ the community sees the "glory" of God. The phrase "becoming flesh" in John's Gospel refers not simply to the human conception of Jesus but to the entire reality of his human existence: his words, his relationships, his healings, his selfless service, his sufferings, and his Death.

For John's Gospel, Jesus is the definitive revealer of God: "No one has ever seen God. The only Son, God, who is at the Father's side, has revealed him" (John 1:18). That conviction echoes throughout the New Testament writings. Other key texts that fashion this conviction are found, for example, in the opening words of the Letter to the Hebrews: "In times past, God spoke in partial and various ways to our ancestors through the prophets; in these last days, he spoke to us through a son, whom he made heir of all things and through whom he created the universe, / who is the refulgence of his glory, / the very imprint of his being, / and who sustains all things by his mighty word" (Hebrews 1:1–3).

5. Finally, the Word embodied in Jesus Christ, a Word expressed in his teaching and compassionate healing, in his gathering of a community, in his giving of his life in the fullness of love, in his conquering of death and his return to communion with the Father for all time—this full articulation of God's Word of redeeming love for the world—is now entrusted to the Apostles and their successors and,

indeed, to the entire Christian community. Fired by the Spirit of God sent upon the Church by the Risen and triumphant Christ, the apostolic Church is commissioned to proclaim the Word of God to the world and, in the spirit of that Word, to form communities of life gathered in the name of Jesus and destined to be witnesses of God's redeeming love for the world to the "ends of the earth." Here is the ultimate basis and the dynamic power for the Church's preaching of the Gospel and for the Scriptures that would flow from and express this proclamation in various ways.

The Beauty and Power of the Word Portrayed within the Bible

This theology of the Word of God is found not simply in official Church statements but also in a passionate way within the Bible itself. The motif of God's Word twists through the entire story of Israel like a powerful sinew. From the creating Word of God in the opening chapters of Genesis to the healing Word of the Lamb who was slain in the Book of Revelation, the Bible is convinced of the overwhelming and transformative power of God's Word.

This Word of God that shaped the universe and shapes the human heart pushes out into history, forging a people and giving them a destiny. God's Word has a particularly transformative impact on the leaders and teachers of God's people: in addition to anointing the kings and emboldening the prophets, it ultimately lays the groundwork for the Church's own mission. So it is with all of the great characters who form the biblical saga; men and women who are hesitant and awkward, unlikely vessels of God, yet summoned by God's compelling and all-powerful Word. They take up their mission on behalf of the people by leading them out of Egypt and slavery, sustaining them in their desert trek, bringing them into the land of promise, purifying them in their failure, comforting them in exile, bringing them back home.

The words of Isaiah 55:10–11, quoted in *Dei Verbum*, beautifully describe the fruitfulness of God's creative word:

> Yet just as from the heavens
> > the rain and snow come down
> And do not return there
> > till they have watered earth,
> > making it fertile and fruitful,
> Giving seed to the one who sows
> > and bread to the one who eats,
> So shall my word be
> > that goes forth from my mouth;
> It shall not return to me empty,
> > but shall do what pleases me,
> > achieving the end for which I sent it.

As we saw earlier, the Jewish Scriptures summed up the Pentateuch—and later, extension, the whole of Scripture—as God's "Law." This is the Law given to Moses with drama and solemnity at Sinai (Exodus 19) and the same Law of Moses that drove movements of reform, such as that of King Josiah in the seventh century (reigned 640–609 BC) and the restoration of Judah under Ezra and Nehemiah.[3] An important point, especially for Christians unfamiliar with Jewish experience, is that the Law was viewed by Israel as God's revelation, as a powerful, guiding, and loving Word that led to life. Obedience to God's Law, God's Word, was not a legalistic experience, but rather a loving response to God's fidelity. A segment of Psalm 19 captures this spirit in beautiful terms:

> The law of the LORD is perfect,
> > refreshing the soul.
> The decree of the LORD is trustworthy,
> > giving wisdom to the simple.
> The precepts of the LORD are right,
> > rejoicing the heart.

---

3   See chapter 2.

More desirable than gold,
　　than a hoard of purest gold,
Sweeter also than honey
　　or drippings from the comb.
(Psalm 19:8–9, 11)

The New Testament's Reflection on Jesus as God's Word

The Word of God—dynamic, powerful, awesome, filled with startling creativity and beauty—that is the sense that Israel had of God's immanent presence in the midst of their history, which paves the way for Christian reflection on the mystery of Jesus as God's Word incarnate and, indeed, as a revelation of the mystery of the Trinity itself.

In the New Testament, God's Word becomes synonymous with Christ and the Christian message. Jesus, the Risen Christ, embodies all that God's Word meant to Israel, all that was revealed through the history of God's people Israel and through the beauty of nature and human wisdom. Jesus *is* the Word that the early Christian community both experienced in its worship and proclaimed through its preaching, as well as in the writings of the New Testament that flowed from that experience. John's Gospel makes this point so eloquently in its prologue, affirming the presence of God's Word at the "beginning"—that is, before all time and space—a Word so perfectly articulated that it reveals God fully (literally: "God is the Word"). Through Jesus, the human embodiment of the Word, the "glory" of God is now revealed.

This same fundamental conviction that Jesus is the embodied Word of God also colors the early Christian language used to describe its mission, a mission that continued Christ's living presence in the world. The early chapters of Acts make this point in a vivid way. Disciples, broken and despairing, are transformed by their encounter with the living Word of the Risen Christ. Peter and the Twelve break out of their room of fear and preach the Word to the crowds of Jewish pilgrims who come to Jerusalem for Pentecost. In the name of Jesus, Peter and John heal the paralyzed man at the Temple gate (Acts 3:1–10). Neither threat nor imprisonment nor flogging can stop the Apostles and their witness to God's Word. A similar point is made in Luke's account of the disciples on the way to Emmaus (Luke 24:13–35). Two disciples flee Jerusalem in despair and sadness, their hopes broken by the Death of Jesus. The mysterious pilgrim who joins them breaks open the power of God's Word and breaks bread with them; their hearts burn within them and they return to the community in Jerusalem.

In a particular way Paul the Apostle exemplified the power of the Word of God in virtually all of his letters. In his bold pastoral plan outlined in Romans, chapter 15, and other passages of his letters, Paul intends to move around the rim of Mediterranean world, through the power of God's Word, planting Christian communities in places no one else has been, thereby making Israel jealous, and finally, triumphantly, handing over the entire world to Christ, who will give it to God. (Paul assumed he would do this in his lifetime!)

For the sake of this mission, Paul thinks of himself as "compelled" to proclaim the Word of God, the Word that is Christ, as expressed in his inexorable logic in Romans 10:12–15, 17.

> For there is no distinction between Jew and Greek; the same Lord is Lord of all, enriching all who call upon him. For "everyone who calls on the name of the Lord will be saved."
>
> But how can they call on him in whom they have not believed? And how can they believe in him of whom they have not heard? And how can they hear without someone to preach? And how can people preach unless they are sent? As it is written, "How beautiful are the feet of those who bring [the] good news!" . . . Thus faith comes from what is heard, and what is heard comes through the word of Christ.

CHAPTER 8

God's Word and the Formation of the Biblical Canon

Both the Jewish community and the early Christian Church believed that God's Word was the source of all creation and was present within their history. The early Christians believed that this same Word was embodied in the person of Jesus Christ, who had died and risen. From these convictions flowed the creation of the biblical canon. The term "canon" comes from the Greek word *kanon*, meaning "rule" or "measuring stick," and its use applied to the Bible had probably originated in Judaism before the advent of Christianity. Simply put, the "biblical canon" refers to those books judged respectively by Judaism and early Christianity to be both sacred and inspired.[1] But the working out of this judgment on the part of both religious traditions was a lengthy and complex process.

The formation of the Christian biblical canon took place over several centuries, culminating officially in the late medieval period. For Catholic Christians the canon was not formally declared until the Council of Trent in 1546. About a decade earlier Martin Luther published his version of the entire Bible and chose the listing of the Old Testament books in accord with the Hebrew canon. This did not mean, however, that until this late medieval period, Christians had been without the Scriptures or unsure of which books belonged to the Bible. For all practical purposes, the canonical books of both Jews and Christians were determined by the end of the second or third centuries AD. And the central core of the Scriptures (that is, the

---

1   See tables listing the books in the various canons in chapter 1, pages 15 –16.

Pentateuch, the writings of the prophets, and the historical books for Judaism; and for Christians, the four Gospels, the Acts of the Apostles, the letters of Paul, and most of the other New Testament writings) was already in place earlier than that.

How was the decision made to accept these particular books and not other sacred writings? And what criteria were used for selection? Here the complexity of the canonical process comes into play. For Judaism, the decision about what books were determined to be inspired and sacred was carried out over a period that began probably around 200 BC. But the formal determination was not made until the first and second centuries AD by various councils of Jewish elders and rabbinic leaders. For Christianity, the decision was also extended and difficult to pinpoint. Apart from the Council of Trent's formal declaration in the sixteenth century there was not a single moment or an express set of criteria that can be pointed to in the formation of the Christian canon. The choice of Old Testament was a rather simple one: the early Church basically accepted the Old Testament books included in the Septuagint or Greek version of the Old Testament—a collection of books that had been formed within Judaism and that served as the "Bible" of the earliest Christian community before any books of the New Testament had come into existence.

The early Church accepted the Old Testament books included in the Septuagint or Greek version of the Old Testament.

Some recent authors have portrayed the canonical process for the selection of the New Testament books as one driven by the combined interests of early Church authorities and, with the appearance of the first Christian Emperor Constantine in the fourth century AD, in alliance with the interests of Roman imperial authority. The suggestion is that this combination of religious and civil authorities chose for inclusion in the New Testament those books that best represented their own interests of orthodoxy and ecclesiastical and civil control, while suppressing other potential sacred books that were viewed as too creative and revolutionary. Such a scenario, made popular even by the 2003 best-selling fiction novel *The Da Vinci Code*, may more accurately reflect modern antiauthoritarian and antiinstitutional sensitivities than it does the complex situation of the first century.

There is little doubt that Church leaders would have an interest—as they should—in which sacred books should be endorsed as inspired and normative for Christian faith. Thus we see that St. Irenaeus, a bishop and theologian living in Gaul (present-day France) in the second half of the

> St. Irenaeus, in the second half of the second century, affirmed a fourfold Gospel over against the gnostics, who claimed they had multiple gospels.

second century, affirmed a fourfold Gospel over against the gnostics, who claimed they had multiple gospels. Irenaeus also admonished those Christians who claimed only one Gospel account. In his famous work, *Adversus Haereses* (*Against Heresies*) Irenaeus noted that the number of the Gospel accounts, four, was providential in that it reflected the four corners of the universe and the four winds created by God.

Irenaeus' critique of those who held to one Gospel account might be in response to the work of Marcion, another second-century Christian theologian, who championed a single Gospel account whose content seems to be close to but not identical with the canonical Gospel of Luke. Marcion also included in his list of biblical books the undisputed letters of Paul, but expressly rejected the Old Testament as representing a God different from the one revealed by Jesus. In fact, Marcion is one of earliest theologians to list something of a "canon" of Scripture. However, his rejection of the Old Testament and choice of only one Gospel account led other Christian leaders to consider his "canon" incomplete and biased against the authentic Jewish roots of the Christian movement. Some historians believe that the appearance of Marcion's list of biblical books actually helped stimulate the formation of the official canon that incorporated the Old as well as the New Testament.

The role of the Emperor Constantine in this process is very murky at best. Some claim that Constantine exerted his influence at the Council of Nicaea (AD 325) to settle on a canonical list. But in fact the Council of Nicaea did not take up the question of the biblical canon at all. Much more important were the deliberations of the Synod of Carthage in 397, some years after the death of Constantine, which confirmed the list of canonical books of both the Old and the New Testament, including a fourfold Gospel.

Thus the theory that ecclesiastical and political pressure to suppress creativity and to maintain control was decisive in the selection of the New Testament books is without any credible basis. Virtually all of the extracanonical "gospels" and other types of religious texts not included in the canon appeared later than the New Testament period. These writings, such as the Gospel of Thomas, the Protoevangelium of James, the Gospel of Mary Magdalene, and the Gospel of Judas, were composed in the second century AD and beyond. Many such texts labeled in the modern era as "gospels" are only fragments rather than complete texts, and many of them are collections of sayings rather than narratives similar to the four canonical Gospels. Some scholars believe that some of the sayings and parables of Jesus that appear in the so-called Gospel of Thomas (it has no Passion narrative) have roots that go back into the first century, but this is hard to prove. Other texts, such as the Gospel of Judas, derive from Coptic Christianity of the late second or early third century, and offer no historical information about Jesus and the circumstances of his life and mission.

The value of such later texts is that they demonstrate the wide diversity of views about Jesus that existed as Christianity moved into the early centuries beyond the New Testament period. Gnosticism, an early Christian heresy that downplayed the humanity of Jesus in favor of his transcendent divine qualities, had a strong influence on several of these texts. The portrayal of Jesus in many of them is far different from the portrayal found in the canonical Gospels and would strike most Christians today as bizarre.

Criteria Guiding the Formation of the New Testament Canon

But what, then, were the criteria that most likely guided the formation of the New Testament canon? Over the years, many scholars have pointed to four criteria that were at work in the early Church's selection of the New Testament books:

1. Apostolic Origin

The connection of the book to either an apostle or someone closely associated with the apostolic generation was one criterion. For example, the authorship of two original Apostles was connected with the Gospel of Matthew and the Gospel of John, respectively. As we noted earlier, we cannot be sure that these two original followers of Jesus were the actual final authors of these Gospels, but it is not unlikely that both Matthew and John were traditionally connected with the communities that produced them. If the motive of the early Church was to simply associate a Gospel with the name of an Apostle, then it is puzzling why it failed to do so for Mark and Luke. In the case of these two Gospels, both figures are associated with Paul as coworkers in his missionary work. Furthermore, concerning Mark, as already noted in chapter 6, the early testimony of the bishop and author Papias (around AD 90) expressly identifies Mark as the author of the Gospel and a close associate of Peter in Rome.[2]

The authorship of two original Apostles was connected with the Gospel of Matthew and the Gospel of John, respectively.

---

2   See chapter 4, page 73.

The other New Testament books also have an apostolic seal of approval, such as the Pauline letters, including the deutero-Pauline letters—that is, those without explicit evidence of his authorship, but clearly related to him—namely 2 Thessalonians, Colossians, Ephesians, and the Pastoral Letters. The Letters of Peter, the Johannine Letters, James, and Jude are all connected with named Apostles. No author's name is found in the Letter to the Hebrews, but in the early centuries of the Church many believed it to be written by Paul. Some, such as the exegete and theologian Origen, doubted it, and modern scholarship is virtually unanimous in its conclusion that Paul was not the author of this anonymous letter. The Book of Revelation identifies its author as "John" (Revelation 1:4, 9) and early tradition assumed this was the Apostle John, although the majority of modern scholars believe that the author is a different John because of the style and theology of the letter.

This criterion of apostolic origin was important because it connected these texts to the very origin of the Christian movement and affirmed authorship that was in close connection with the proclamation of the Risen Christ by the apostolic Church.

2. Universal Acceptance

This criterion is especially important because it takes into account the reception of these texts on the part of the early Christian communities. Those who attribute the formation of the canon mainly to the self-serving decisions of ecclesiastical or civil authorities overlook a much more important source of authority for the canonical books, namely that they were received and approved through their usage by a substantial portion of the early Christian communities. A Gospel or New Testament letter that portrayed the mission of Jesus and his status as the Risen Christ and Savior in a way that was radically different from the apostolic

> The canonical books were received and approved through their usage by a substantial portion of the early Christian communities.

proclamation that formed the foundation of the early Church would not have been acceptable for the majority of Christians.

Another aspect of canonicity, to be taken up later, is inspiration. From the perspective of Christian faith, the inspiration of God's Spirit also plays a role here by initiating, sustaining, and inspiring Christian faith. That collective faith of the early Church, taken in its entirety and including a broad spectrum of the early Christian communities, enabled the Christians to receive and recognize the authenticity of the proclamation found in the four Gospels, the letters of Paul, and the other canonical writings. The great theologian Karl Rahner, one of the architects of the Second Vatican Council, used the image of the Church's "self-consciousness" to describe this criterion.[3] What he meant by that is simply that someone reading their own diary written long ago and perhaps long-forgotten, would still recognize in those writings their own unique consciousness and self-identity. In a certain way, the writings of the New Testament express this "self-consciousness" of the apostolic Church during a period of its vital formation as a community of faith.

Admittedly a few of the books ultimately included in the canon were debated before being finally accepted, such as the Letter to the Hebrews, Jude, and the Book of Revelation. Other nonbiblical texts, too, such as the Didache, the Teaching of the Twelve Apostles, or the Shepherd of Hermas, seem to be on a par with the content and quality of the New Testament books, but were not included; it is difficult to determine why this was so. Nevertheless, the criterion of universal acceptance remains valid and important for the books that did become part of the canon. By the end of the fourth century AD, all of the canonical books of the New Testament fell under this important criterion.

3. Liturgical Use

This criterion is similar to the previous one of "Universal Acceptance." What it adds is the important context in which most of the New

---

3   Karl Rahner, *Inspiration in the Bible* (*Questiones Disputatae*, 1) rev. ed. (New York: Herder and Herder, 1964), 49–52.

Testament texts were originally proclaimed—that is, the common worship of the early Church in general, the Eucharist in particular. The Christians gathered in an atmosphere of common prayer and community celebration (including meals) to hear passages from the Old Testament, passages from one of Paul's letters, and later in the first century, the recitation of part of a Gospel, and then to celebrate the Eucharist together.

This pattern is reflected in Luke's account of the disciples on the road to Emmaus: the Risen Jesus first explains to the two disciples the meaning of the Scriptures and then celebrates a meal with them (Luke 24). In Acts 2:42–47, Luke describes the exuberant life of the early Jerusalem community that devotes itself to "the communal life, to the breaking of the bread and to the prayers." In addition, "every day they devoted themselves to meeting together in the temple area and to breaking bread in their homes. They ate their meals with exaltation and sincerity of heart, praising God and enjoying favor with all the people."

Paul himself describes this sort of gathering in 1 Corinthians 11:17–34. His point is not to describe in any detail the nature of this meal gathering and its rituals, but to stop an abuse. Some of the wealthy members are eating and drinking lavishly while the poorer members go hungry. To drive home his point about how inconsistent this is with what should be the spirit of their gathering, Paul actually cites the account of the Last Supper:

> The Lord Jesus, on the night he was handed over, took bread, and, after he had given thanks, broke it and said, "This is my body that is for you. Do this in remembrance of me." In the same way also the cup, after supper, saying, "This cup is the new covenant in my blood. Do this, as often as you drink it, in remembrance of me." For as often as you eat this bread and drink the cup, you proclaim the death of the Lord until he comes. (1 Corinthians 11:23–26)

The first century Greco-Roman world was accustomed to festive meals. Meetings of various workers' guilds (such as bakers, butchers, merchants) and other voluntary associations often had their meetings at a meal. So, too, civic and familial celebrations took place around meals or banquets. In one sense, the Christians who gathered at meals were simply following a custom of their surrounding culture. But the references to such meals in the New Testament demonstrate that these early Christian meals took on a different and more profound meaning. In the Old Testament Israel celebrated the Passover meal in remembrance of their liberation from slavery and to express their hopes for future redemption. The famous text of Isaiah 25:6–8 (often read at Catholic funerals today) portrays the final consummation of Israel's hopes as a sumptuous meal on Mount Sion:

> On this mountain the LORD of hosts
>> will provide for all peoples
> A feast of rich food and choice wines,
>> juicy, rich food and pure, choice wines.
> On this mountain he will destroy
>> the veil that veils all peoples,
> The web that is woven over all nations.
>> He will destroy death forever.
> The Lord GOD will wipe away
>> the tears from all faces;
> The reproach of his people he will remove
>> from the whole earth; for the LORD has spoken.

There is no doubt Jesus himself made meals a hallmark of his ministry, especially welcoming those on the perimeter of society. In its liturgy and in its theology, the Church has always traced the Institution of the Eucharist to that poignant meal on the eve of Jesus' Death. Gathered with his disciples, with death staring him in the face, Jesus broke bread and shared the cup with his earnest but troubled followers. Although biblical scholarship has long debated what the precise nature of this meal was in its original setting, the synoptic Gospels clearly place it in the context of Passover (Mark 14:12; Matthew 26:17; Luke 22:7–8). In the spirit of the Passover, the Gospel tradition made this a meal deeply embedded in biblical memory, a meal that evoked a history of great suffering, but also a hope projected into the future—"next year in Jerusalem."

It was not only the rich aura of Passover that entwined the Last Supper account and opened the doors to a flood of biblical memories for the early Christians. Indeed, the Last Supper reverberated with a series of remarkable meals that Jesus had celebrated throughout his public ministry and had made the settings of several of his parables. Although Luke's Gospel in particular emphasizes this feature of Jesus' ministry, it is present in all four of the Gospel accounts: Jesus' calling of the toll collector Levi to be a disciple and then dining in his house with a crowd of "tax collectors and sinners" (Matthew 9:9–13; Mark 2:13–17; Luke 5:27–32); Jesus eating with his disciples in Simon Peter's house at Capernaum after restoring his mother-in-law to health (Matthew 8:14–15; Mark 1:29–31; Luke 4:38–39); Jesus dining with Simon the Pharisee when a woman of the city breaks in and anoints Jesus' feet with precious ointment, bathing them with her tears and drying them with her hair (Luke 7:36–50); Jesus calling for food to be served to Jairus' daughter, when she had been drawn back from the very valley of death (Mark 5:42; Luke 8:55); and Jesus with Zacchaeus, chief tax collector of Jericho and a rich man, after Jesus spots him in the Sycamore tree (Luke 19:1–10).

> Indeed, the Last Supper reverberated with a series of remarkable meals that Jesus had celebrated throughout his public ministry.

The parables of Jesus are also filled with meal images. The Kingdom of Heaven is imagined as a great banquet, the table laden with food and drink, and in place of the guests who balked at coming, invitations are sent out to the highways and the byways, and the banquet hall is filled with the poor, the disabled, the outsiders, and the unclean (Matthew 22:1–14; Luke 14:15–24). A banquet is imagined by Jesus in which many Gentiles come from east and west and take their place at table with Abraham, and Isaac and Jacob (Matthew

8:11–12). A banquet celebrates the return of a lost son and causes resentment in the heart of the one who had never left (Luke 15:11–32).

In one of the most remarkable texts of the Gospel accounts, found in both Matthew and Luke, Jesus reflects back to his opponents their hostile image of him, comparing himself to John the Baptist: "For John the Baptist came neither eating food nor drinking wine, and you said, 'He is possessed by a demon.' The Son of Man came eating and drinking and you said, 'Look, he is a glutton and a drunkard, a friend of tax collectors and sinners'" (Luke 7:33–34; nearly identical wording is found in Matthew 11:19). This is truly an extraordinary text that confirms that meals were a hallmark of Jesus' ministry and a commentary on his vision of God's reign.

And, of course, no scene drives this home more forcefully than the account of Jesus' feeding of the multitudes found in all four Gospel accounts (Mark 6:32–44; 8:1–10; Matthew 14:13–21; 15:32–39; Luke 9:10–17; John 6:1–13). These feedings of thousands of hungry people in the desolate areas of Galilee are dramatic and powerful signs of Jesus' mission, and they attract with magnetic force so many of the master images of biblical history. The stage is set in the "wilderness," the *eremos topos*, deliberately recalling God's feeding of the Israelites with manna during their desert trek (Exodus 16). The scant provisions to satisfy so much hunger—a few loaves and a few fish—also recalled the great prophetic ministries of Elijah, who miraculously saved a widow and her son (1 Kings 17:7–24) and Elisha who fed one hundred people with twenty barley loaves (2 Kings 4:42–44).

The evangelists linked these great meals, laden with so many powerful biblical memories, to the Last Supper of Jesus, the final Passover, that in turn would serve as the master symbol of the Christian Eucharist (compare, for example, Mark 6:41 and 14:22).

Thus the criterion of "Liturgical Use" was a key element in the Church's discernment of which New Testament books should be included in the canon. Texts worthy of being read in the setting of the Eucharist reflected the teaching and spirit of the Risen Christ known instinctively to the community of faith. As Matthew Levering puts it: "Scripture is most itself when proclaimed in the Eucharistic liturgy, because in the liturgy God is drawing us into the realities that Scripture describes."[4]

4. Consistent Message

Even though the portrayal of Jesus is different in each of the Gospel accounts, there is still a profound unity that binds those portrayals together. John's depiction of Jesus as the Word made flesh is different than the portrait found in Mark or Matthew or Luke, but it is not contrary to their portrayal of the Jesus who proclaims the coming Reign of God. Paul's image for the Church as "Christ's body" (found at 12:27) is different in language and tone than the emphasis in the Letter of James on the Church as an assembly that must welcome the poor. It is different but not contrary to it. And thus a case can be made with integrity that the writings of the New Testament, taken as a whole, give a consistent affirmation of Christian faith in Jesus Christ as the exalted Son of God and affirm a consistent description of the demands of Christian discipleship.

All four of these criteria were in play in subtle and diffuse ways as the early Church sorted through its collective decision about which books were inspired and sacred, and therefore belonged in the canon. Within the entirety of the canon of Scripture—both the Old and the New Testament—was to be found the faith of the Church, guided by the very Spirit with which the Risen Christ had endowed the Church.

---

4   Matthew Levering, *Engaging the Doctrine of Revelation: The Mediation of the Gospel through Church and Scripture* (Grand Rapids: Baker Academic, 2014), 85.

The Rationale of the Canonical Order

As we have noted, the order of the Old Testament canonical books within the Christian canon was determined by the order found within the Septuagint. The fourfold division of the Old Testament books in the Catholic canon (Pentateuch, Historical Books, Wisdom Books, and Prophetic Books—see the chart on page 16) concludes with the book of Malachi, a prophetic text whose vision is turned to the future liberation of Israel and was thus read by the early Christians as preparation for the coming of Christ.

Determining the precise rationale of the order of the New Testament books is more challenging. Clearly the four Gospel accounts are presented first because they portray the life of Jesus, the heart of the Christian faith. The order among the four accounts—Matthew, Mark, Luke, and John—probably represents what early generations of Christians thought was the chronological order, although modern biblical scholarship is convinced from internal evidence that Mark's Gospel was first, both in chronology and as a primary source of Matthew and Luke.

> Clearly the four Gospel accounts are presented first because they portray the life of Jesus, the heart of the Christian faith.

Even though the Acts of the Apostles was probably written in tandem with Luke's Gospel as a two-volume work, in the canon it comes after John's Gospel because the four Gospel accounts were to be presented together. The placement of Acts may also determine a certain preparation for the remaining New Testament books, in that many of the great apostolic figures mentioned in Acts are represented in the other New Testament books that follow it. Paul's letters come first, including those that modern biblical scholarship judged to be "deutero-Pauline," or not of Paul's direct authorship, (that is, 2 Thessalonians, Colossians, Ephesians, and the pastoral letters: 1 Timothy, 2 Timothy, and Titus). Philemon, an authentic but very brief letter of Paul, follows these texts. The canon seems to sort out

Paul's letters by first listing those written to communities: Romans, 1 Corinthians, 2 Corinthians, Galatians, Ephesians, Philippians, Colossians, 1 Thessalonians, and 2 Thessalonians, as well as then those addressed to individuals: 1 Timothy, 2 Timothy, Titus, and Philemon. Within the two categories the letters seemed to be ranked by their length (although Ephesians is slightly longer than Galatians!). Hebrews brings up the rear of the Pauline list since even in the early centuries of the Church Paul's authorship of this text was questioned.

Next in order are the so-called "Catholic letters" (also listed according to size: James, 1 Peter, 2 Peter, 1 John, 2 John, 3 John, and Jude). The Book of Revelation provides an appropriate finale to the New Testament canon. All of the authors assigned to these New Testament books are mentioned in the Acts of the Apostles. Thus in the canonical order, Acts serves as a bridge between the life of Jesus portrayed in the four Gospels and the life of the apostolic Church presented in the Acts itself and in a diffuse way by the other writings of the New Testament.

The Remaining New Testament Books: The Catholic Letters and the Apocalypse

The Gospels, the Acts of the Apostles, and the Pauline Letters are the heart of the New Testament, the Scriptures most heavily represented in the selections of the Lectionary, and the ones that most deeply affect Christian devotion. We have commented briefly on the deutero-Pauline letters attributed to Paul, as well as Hebrews and the Johannine letters.[5] What remains are the so-called "Catholic Letters" (James, 1 and 2 Peter, and Jude) and the Apocalypse or Book of Revelation. These books add to the remarkable literary and theological diversity of the New Testament and underscore the criterion of "apostolic origin" that paved their way into the canon. The limits of space do

---

5   For Hebrews, see pages 58–59; for the Johannine letters, see pages 90–91.

not allow any elaborate treatment of these New Testament books, but some comment on their place within the canon is important.

The Catholic Letters are so named because they are not addressed to a particular community or individual but to a more general audience; the meaning of "catholic" in this instance refers to "universal." However, the First Letter of Peter addresses several specific communities in north and central Asia Minor and was apparently intended to be something of a circular letter to them (see 1 Peter 1:1).

The Letter of James comes first in the canonical order of these letters. The author identifies himself as "James, a slave of God and of the Lord Jesus Christ" who writes to "the twelve tribes in the dispersion" (James 1:1), most likely referring to James, the "brother of the Lord" (Galatians 1:19)—a relative of Jesus himself and a leader of the Jerusalem church (see Acts 15:13–21). The "twelve tribes in the dispersion" is used metaphorically to refer to the Jewish Christian communities addressed and would make most sense if the author were writing from Jerusalem. Is James the actual author? Or, as in the case of the deutero-Pauline letters, is he a later disciple writing in the name of James? Scholars are divided on this issue. If the historical James of Jerusalem is the author—which cannot be ruled out—then the letter would date to the late 50s or early 60s. It is estimated that James died as a martyr around AD 62.[6] The letter takes the form of a moral exhortation, drawing deeply on Jewish moral traditions as amplified by Jesus himself.

Two letters are attributed to the Apostle Peter, but each is quite different. The First Letter of Peter is one of the most beautiful among the New Testament letters. The author identifies himself as "Peter, an apostle of Jesus Christ" (1:1).

> The First Letter of Peter is one of the most beautiful among the New Testament letters.

Here, too, there is considerable debate whether the historical Peter actually wrote the letter. Some scholars conclude that the fine Greek

---

6   Josephus, *Antiquities of the Jews*, book 20, chapter 9.1.

style of the letter and the situation it assumes about the communities addressed would make it unlikely that Peter, the Palestinian disciple of Jesus, was the author. One solution suggested in recent times is that this letter (and perhaps 2 Peter as well) originated from a "Petrine circle" or group of leaders who had been very familiar with Peter and wrote in his name following his martyrdom in Rome. If the letter was written by the historical Peter then it would have to be dated sometime in the early 60s, prior to the Apostle's martyrdom under Nero. If, as may be more probable, the letter comes from this Petrine group writing to a number of churches already well-established in north and central Asia Minor, then it should be dated to sometime in the last quarter of the first century.

The Second Letter of Peter is different in tone and content. It, too, presents itself as written by "Symeon Peter, a slave and apostle of Jesus Christ" (2 Peter 1:1) and even refers to Peter's experience of the Transfiguration of Jesus (1:17–18). Despite this, most scholars believe it was written by a later disciple, perhaps from the same circle suggested for 1 Peter. The author of 2 Peter is aware of the earlier letter (3:1). And he refers to Paul's letters. In warning that "the ignorant and unstable" may distort some things in those letters that are difficult to understand, he adds "just as they do the other scriptures" (3:16), indicating a status that would have been given to Paul's writings only later in the first century. Also 2 Peter, chapters 2–3 appears to borrow heavily from the Letter of Jude.[7]

These factors suggest that with 2 Peter we are coming close to the end of the New Testament canon. The author uses the authoritative voice of the revered Apostle Peter to sustain the community's faith and its trust in the truth of the Scriptures and the early Christian tradition.

Listed last among the Catholic Letters (probably because of its brevity) is the Letter of Jude. Here again the remarkable diversity of

---

7   See, for example, the similarities between Jude 6 and 2 Peter 2:4. Most commentators believe 2 Peter copied from Jude rather than the other way around.

the books included in the New Testament canon is on display. The text wears the format of a letter very lightly—it is more like a sermon or exhortation. The author identifies himself as "Jude, a slave of Jesus Christ and brother of James" (Jude 1 probably refers to Jude, the brother of the Lord mentioned as Judas in Mark 6:3, also Matthew 13:55, as one of the "brothers" of Jesus residing in Nazareth). The frequent use of Old Testament quotations and examples in Jude, plus the citation of other nonbiblical Jewish texts such as 1 Enoch (Jude 6, 14–15) and the Assumption of Moses (Jude 9) give the letter a strong Jewish-Christian flavor. The main concern of the author is similar to that of others writing later in the New Testament period: to warn the community in no uncertain terms of "intruders" and "godless persons" whose doctrinal errors and perverse lifestyle are a threat to the peace and fidelity of the believers.

Apocalypsis, the Greek form of "Apocalypse," literally means "revelation."

The Revelation to John (sometimes known as the Book of Revelation or the Apocalypse; *apocalypsis*, the Greek form of "Apocalypse," literally means "revelation") is, appropriately, the final book in the New Testament canon. Its use of heavenly visions, vivid symbols and dramatic images to convey its message reflects an apocalyptic literary style found in other Jewish texts of the period, making it challenging for modern readers to interpret its precise meaning. The author identifies himself as "John" (see Revelation 1:4, 9) and has been traditionally identified with the Apostle John, who was believed to have also composed the Gospel according to John.[8] However, the completely different style and perspective of Revelation has led modern biblical scholarship to doubt that the author is the same as the Evangelist John. The John of this text is apparently in exile on the Mediterranean island of Patmos because of his fearless witness to Christ (1:9). There he has a powerful visionary experience that compels him to compose this book (1:19). Its portrayal of Roman imperial

---

8   See chapter 4 pages 84–92.

might and the distress of Christian communities in Asia Minor that fell under the sway of Rome fits the circumstances in Asia Minor in the last decades of the first century.

The fundamental scenario of the Book of Revelation is the clash between the forces of evil—identified with Rome and the blasphemous claims of its rulers—and the power of the Lamb, the Crucified, Risen, and Exalted Christ. In contrast to the forces of evil who use violence and economic exploitation to impose their rule over humans (see the excoriation of Rome's economic exploitation in chapter 18), the Lamb "that was slain" (5:12) represents the holiness and sacrificial love of Christ. The triumph of the Lamb and its consequences form the conclusion of Revelation (21:1—22:5). The new Jerusalem comes down from heaven and renews the earth, bringing light, beauty, and peace to those who have been faithful.

Many interpreters over the centuries have viewed the Book of Revelation as a prophecy of specific historical events that would take place at the end of the world, but it is clear that Revelation is addressed first of all to the Christians of the first century who suffered under Roman rule and who were perplexed at how to respond. The theological perspective of the Book of Revelation has enduring value—Christians must remain faithful to the Gospel even in the midst of distress; the final destiny of humanity and the created world will not be overwhelmed by the forces of evil and violence but by the loving and creative power of God revealed in Christ the Lamb. This is the final message with which the Christian canon concludes.

The theological perspective of the Book of Revelation has enduring value—Christians must remain faithful to the Gospel even in the midst of distress.

CHAPTER 9

The Inspiration and Truth of the Bible

The early Church included in the canon of the New Testament those books they considered both sacred and "inspired." What is meant by biblical inspiration? Two New Testament texts themselves refer to the Scriptures as "inspired": the author of 2 Timothy states: "All scripture is inspired by God and is useful for teaching, for refutation, for correction, and for training in righteousness, so that one who belongs to God may be competent, equipped for every good work" (3:16–17). The Second Letter of Peter warns about misinterpretation of the Scriptures: "Know this first of all, that there is no prophecy of scripture that is a matter of personal interpretation, for no prophecy ever came through human will; but rather human beings moved by the holy Spirit spoke under the influence of God" (2 Peter 1:20–21). Each text uses a different term to refer to "inspiration"— "inspired by God" (*theopneustos*) in 2 Timothy and "moved by the holy Spirit" (*hupo pneumatos hagiou pheromenoi*) in 2 Peter—but both affirm a similar conviction. The "scriptures" (*hai graphai*) referred to are most likely the Old Testament, since at this early date it is unlikely that these letters would be referring to the Gospels or Paul's letters as the "scriptures."

But these texts do express a conviction of the early Church that the biblical writings were "inspired." Viewing the Scriptures from the vantage point of faith, the early Church considered these sacred texts as truly the "Word of God." From one point of view, the notion of "inspiration" is identical with the concept of "revelation." But "biblical inspiration" refers to a more specific instance of revelation, namely the biblical *writings*. As the biblical scholar Denis Farkasfalvy has noted:

> The study of biblical inspiration in its strict and proper sense begins at the point where we focus on a specific question: How, when, and why did God's revelatory word become stable and permanent as a text in written form, which was then ready to be redacted, edited, and transmitted from generation to generation under the auspices of a community of believers and its leadership. [1]

Implied in this description of inspiration is a further distinction that theologians have made, that is, between "objective inspiration"—the particular *writings* that are considered "inspired"—and "subjective inspiration," referring to the influence of the Holy Spirit on the *writers* who were responsible for composing the biblical books.

The Second Vatican Council took up this issue in *Dei Verbum, Dogmatic Constitution on Divine Revelation*. The Council affirmed, in paragraph 11, what was the consistent teaching of the Church:

> Those things revealed by God which are contained and presented in the text of sacred scripture have been written under the inspiration of the holy Spirit. For holy mother church, relying on the faith of the apostolic age, accepts as sacred and canonical the books of the Old and New Testaments, whole and entire, with all their parts, on the grounds that, written under the inspiration of the holy Spirit (see Jn 20:31; 2 Tim 3:16; 2 Pet 1:19–21; 3:15–16) they have God as their author, and have been handed on as such to the church itself. [2] To compose the sacred books, God chose certain men who, all the while he employed them in this task, made full use of their powers and faculties [3] so that, though he had

---

1 Denis Farkasfalvy, OCIST, *Inspiration & Interpretation: A Theological Introduction to Sacred Scripture* (Washington DC: Catholic University of America Press, 2010), 208.

2 See Vatican Council I, Dogmatic Constitution on the Catholic Faith, *Dei Filius*, ch. 2: Denz. 1787 (3006). Pontifical Biblical Commission, Decree 18 June 1915: Denz. 20180 (3629); EB 420. Holy Office, Letter, 22 Dec. 1923: EB 499.

3 See Pius XII, Encyclical *Divino Afflante Spiritu*, 30 Sept. 1943: AAS 35 (1943), p. 314; EB 556. ibid: EB 569.

acted in them and by them,[4] it was as true authors that they consigned to writing whatever he wanted written, and no more.[5]

Several important components of the Church's teaching on biblical inspiration are found here. First and foremost, it affirms that God is the ultimate "author" of the Scriptures. Catholic teaching makes clear that God is not the "author" in the normal sense of the term—put bluntly, God did not write the letter to Philemon. Rather, God is the "author" in the sense that God is the origin and dynamic power that drives the events contained in the Scriptures and moves the human authors to eventually put these biblical accounts into writing.

Second, the Council also affirms that the biblical writers are "true authors" in every sense of the term. This is a key point. Acknowledging that the human authors of the Bible are "true authors" makes room for all the realities of human authorship: the limits and merits of the particular culture, time, language, and the social, religious, and political contexts that influence human authors in any age. This human dimension of the Scriptures also provides the basis for historical-critical scholarship that has characterized biblical studies over the past couple of centuries, including, as we noted earlier, the strong involvement of Catholic scholars.

Acknowledging that the human authors of the Bible are "true authors" makes room for all the realities of human authorship.

Trying to understand how both the divine origin of the Scriptures and human authorship come together, has been and continues to be a subject of theological debate. For those who discount any special "inspired" quality in the Bible, this subject is of little interest. For the community of faith that believes in the unique and normative character of the Scriptures, this is an important question.

---

4   In and through human beings: see Heb 1:1 and 4:7 (in); 2 Kg 23:2; Mt 1:22 and passim (through); Vatican Council I, Scheme on Catholic Doctrine, note 9: *Collectio Lacensis*, VII, 522.

5   See Leo XIII, Enclyclical *Providentissimus Deus*: EB 114; Benedict XV, Encyclical *Spiritus Paraclitius*: EB 483.

Drawing on the categories of traditional philosophy, one way of describing the process of "subjective inspiration" (that is, as noted above, the process by which the biblical writers themselves are inspired by the Holy Spirit) was to use the categories of "causality." In this perspective, God would be the "first cause" as the source of the Scriptures while the human author is the "instrumental" cause who, as the text from *Dei Verbum* asserts, "consigned to writing whatever he [God] wanted written and no more." An analogy illustrating "instrumental causality" would be that of a writer (the first cause) and his or her pen (the instrumental cause) that traces exactly the input of the writer. In this instance, the writer exercises his or her authorship and the pen acts completely as a pen should.

This view of biblical inspiration is illustrated in a number of classical paintings depicting the Evangelists writing their Gospel accounts. I have a copy of such a painting on my office wall: St. Matthew sits at his writing desk, quill pen in hand; standing over his shoulder and dictating word by word is an angel (the Holy Spirit)! However, there are several problems with this conception of biblical inspiration. Seeing the biblical author as analogous to a pen or "instrument" guided by God, and inspiration as a kind of divine dictation, does not leave enough room for the biblical writers as "true authors." They might be considered "true secretaries" but not "true authors," who are fully engaged in the composition of the biblical text.

If, in effect, God "dictated" the Bible word for word, we are faced with the difficulty of explaining all of the human limitations that are evident in the biblical writings, a topic we will turn to next. How do we explain the violence found in the Scriptures, or the erroneous assumptions about the composition of the universe, or the causes of illness, to name just a few cases.[6] Such an explanation of biblical inspiration tends to make the Bible a "magical" book dropped down from heaven that overlooks its human dimensions.

Another challenge to the type of explanation illustrated in the Evangelist portrait on my wall is that it assumes that each of the biblical books was written by a single author at a particular point in time. As we have seen, however, with the exception of Paul's letters and some other New Testament letters, the composition of most of the biblical books was a protracted and complex process, involving in some instances generations of unnamed teachers and leaders and prophets who transmitted, edited, and reinterpreted the traditions ultimately put into writing in the biblical books. Even the Gospel accounts themselves drew on material that had first been formulated and shaped by the living tradition of the early Church. The names of the apostolic authors assigned to the Gospels in the second century, such as Matthew or John, may in fact not have identified the final editor who put into writing the version of the Gospels we know today. This does not mean that the Gospels and the other biblical books were written by a committee. One can trace, for example, the particular style of each evangelist, and on the basis of vocabulary and style and content, scholars distinguish between Paul's "undisputed" letters and those that are "deutero-Pauline"—that is, written later by a disciple of Paul.

To affirm that the Spirit inspires the biblical authors means that the process (or gift) of inspiration was at work—not only in individual authors among the people of Israel and the early Church, but also that the Spirit guided and informed the entire process and the myriads of people that led to the ultimate written composition of the

> The composition of most of the biblical books was a protracted and complex process.

---

6   The Pontifical Biblical Commission's statement, *The Inspiration and Truth of Sacred Scripture*, devotes an entire section to such issues as violence, extermination warfare, prayers for vengeance, suffering, and the status of women; see pages 143–156.

Scriptures. Some modern theologians have referred to this perspective as a "social" theory of inspiration.

Theologians still struggle to come up with a fully satisfying and intelligent explanation for the process of inspiration. This does not mean that inspiration is an illusion, but simply that we are dealing with a profound reality. It is possible by way of analogy to compare the mystery of the divine and human in the inspired Scriptures to other Christian mysteries where the divine and human are fused, such as the Incarnation itself or in the Eucharistic transformation of the elements of bread and wine into the Body and Blood of Christ. Pope Benedict XVI, in his apostolic exhortation *The Word of the Lord*, makes this very point in speaking of inspiration: "Here too we can suggest an analogy: as the word of God became flesh by the power of the Holy Spirit in the womb of the Virgin Mary, so sacred Scripture is born from the womb of the Church by the power of the same Spirit."[7]

The Truth of the Bible

A consequence of *Dei Verbum*'s affirmation that the Scriptures are "inspired" and have God as their ultimate "author" or source leads to another aspect of this teaching—the Bible is true in its entirety. This is often referred to as the "inerrancy" of the Scriptures. The Council itself drew this conclusion:

> Since, therefore, all that the inspired authors, or sacred writers, affirm should be regarded as affirmed by the holy Spirit, we must acknowledge that the books of scripture, firmly, faithfully, and without error, teach that truth which God, for the sake of our salvation, wished to see confided to the sacred scriptures. (*Dei Verbum*, 11)

Here again this Catholic teaching has to be understood in a thoughtful way. The "truth" of the Scriptures does not mean that every statement in the Bible is true in every way, nor even that the events included in the Bible must be historical in every sense of the

---

7   *The Word of the Lord (Verbum Domini)*, 19.

term. The Council text affirms this in the paragraph immediately following its assertion that the Scriptures are "without error" by insisting that biblical interpretation has to take into account the limitations of human authorship in the Bible.[8]

The truth of the Bible, from a Catholic standpoint, means that in the entirety of the Scriptures the full truth of God's providence and saving grace is faithfully proclaimed. The phrase "for the sake of our salvation" was a key element of the Council's teaching on this matter. The Council fathers did not want to say that *parts* of the Scripture contain this truth and others do not; no, the Bible has an overall cohesion, as we have noted in reviewing the formation of the canon. There are, of course, assertions in the Scriptures (for example, the creation of the universe in seven days as in Genesis 1, or that human conception takes place by a "mingling of blood" as in John 1:13) that do not hold up to later scientific inquiry, and some events included in the Bible may not be "historical" in the sense we would use the term today (for example, Jonah's sojourn in the belly of the sea monster or the arrival of the Hebrews into Canaan in a single dramatic journey). At the same time there *are* many significant historical events narrated in the Bible, such as the Assyrian invasion in the ninth century BC or the historical Jesus of Nazareth who lived in first century Roman Palestine. What the Council and the long tradition of Catholic teaching affirms is that there is a divine dimension to the whole of the inspired Scriptures and this divine dimension guarantees that the Scriptures gift us with "that truth which God, for the sake of our salvation, wished to see confided to the sacred scriptures."[9]

---

8   *Dei Verbum*, par. 12: "Rightly to understand what the sacred authors wanted to affirm in their work, due attention must be paid both to the customary and characteristic patterns of perception, speech and narrative which prevailed in their time, and to the conventions which people then observed in their dealings with one another. [Pius XII, loc. cit.: Denz. 2294 (3829–3830); EB 557–562.]"

9   Ibid., 11.

Conclusion: The Scriptures—
God's Inspired Word of Salvation

These affirmations of Catholic teaching about the formation of the canon and about biblical inspiration and the truth of the Bible do not solve all of the theological issues on exactly how this takes place. There will continue to be debate about all of this. What is clear, however, is that the community of faith recognizes a profound spiritual or theological dimension of the Bible that makes the Scriptures unique and normative (that is, setting the authentic pattern for Christian life). The powerful and life-giving Word of God comes to us both in the Scriptures themselves and in the ongoing Tradition of the Church, which, through the power of the Spirit, is called to live in accord with the biblical Word and is entrusted with its authentic interpretation.

GLOSSARY

Apocryphal From the Greek word for "hidden;" understood to mean "of doubtful authenticity."

Canon From the Greek *kannon*, meaning "rule" or "measuring stick"; those books judged respectively by Judaism and early Christianity to be both sacred and inspired.

Deutero From the Greek word for "second," thus anything described with "deutero" as the prefix indicates something "secondary." The deutero-Pauline letters are those likely written by a disciple in his name after Paul's lifetime (as opposed to those for which strong evidence exists that Paul wrote them).

Deuteronomist Source One of the sources identified in the composition of the Pentateuch.

Dualism A position that tends to see contrasting elements as clear-cut opposites that never overlap.

Elohist Source One of the sources identified as contributing to the composition of the Pentateuch.

Epistle From the Greek *epistole*, meaning "letter" and used to refer to the Pauline and other New Testament letters.

Greco-Roman The term refers to the foundational role that Greek culture and language had in the Mediterranean world from the time of Alexander the Great (356–323 BC) through the period of the Roman Empire (47 BC–AD 394), which perpetuated many aspects of Greek culture. Characteristics include: the Greek language; a consciousness of the role of the city as an economic and cultural center; love of sports and the cult of the body (for example, the gymnasium, the race track); greater attention to the individual within the bonds of the community; and a history of art and theatre.

Hellenistic Related to Greek culture spread by Alexander's empire and influential in the Mediterranean from approximately 323 to 31 BC.

Inerrancy A doctrine that affirms the fundamental truth of the Bible.

Inspiration A doctrine that affirms that the various writers of the biblical books were guided or "inspired" by the Holy Spirit.

Johannine Texts related (either directly or indirectly) to the historical figure, John the Evangelist.

Ketuvim A Hebrew word for "writings" usually referring to the various biblical books included in the third segment of the Hebrew Bible, after the "Law" and the "Prophets."

Masoretic Text Drawn from a Hebrew word that refers to the transmission of a tradition, the "Masoretic text" is the authoritative version of the Hebrew Bible.

Neviim From the Hebrew word for "prophets" this term is also used to describe the second major portion of the Hebrew Bible.

Pentateuch From the Greek word for "five" and referring to the first five books of the Bible.

Priestly Source One of the sources detected as contributing to the composition of the Pentateuch, or first five books of the Bible.

Q From the German word *Quelle* or "source." Used by scholars to designate a hypothetical source for material found in Matthew and Luke, but not in Mark. No independent copies of "Q" are known to exist.

Rabbinic Judaism A generic term referring to the formative stage of Jewish life that emerged after the destruction of the Temple in

AD 70 when, under the leadership of rabbis and sages, Judaism reorganized and renewed itself. This period is foundational for the character of Jewish life as we know it today.

Revelation A generic term referring to God's self-revelation through the Scriptures, within history, and through the authoritative teaching of the Church.

Synoptic Gospel Accounts The Greek word means "seeing together"; Matthew, Mark, and Luke share many episodes and sayings in their accounts of the life of Jesus Christ, whereas John's account contains much content distinctive from the other three.

Tanak A term describing the Hebrew Bible, formed by the first letters of the Hebrew names for each of its three major sections: the Torah, the Prophets, and the Writings.

Torah From the Hebrew word "teaching" or "law" and applied to the totality of the first five books of the Bible.

Tradition A set of beliefs and practices handed down within a group or society that takes on special authoritative importance. In Catholicism "Tradition" can refer in a formal sense to the authoritative teachings of the Church that together with Scripture proclaim and amplify God's Word.

Yahwist Source One of the several sources detected in the composition of the Pentateuch.

FOR FURTHER READING—
A SELECTIVE LIST

American Bible Society. *Synopsis of the Four Gospels*. Rev. standard version. New York: American Bible Society, 2010.

Benedict XVI. *The Word of the Lord. Verbum Domini*. Washington, DC: United States Conference of Catholic Bishops Publications, 2010.

Cameron, Michael. *Unfolding Sacred Scripture: How Catholics Read the Bible*. Chicago: Liturgy Training Publications, 2015.

Dunn, James D. G. *Jesus, Paul, and the Gospels*. Grand Rapids, MI: Eerdmans, 2011.

Eve, Eric. *Behind the Gospels: Understanding the Oral Tradition*. Minneapolis, MN: Fortress, 2014.

Farkasfalvy, Denis, OCIST. *Inspiration & Interpretation: A Theological Introduction to Sacred Scripture*. Washington, DC: Catholic University of America Press, 2010.

Levering, Matthew. *Engaging the Doctrine of Revelation: The Mediation of the Gospel through Church and Scripture*. Grand Rapids, MI: Baker Academic, 2014.

McDonald, Lee Martin. *Formation of the Bible: The Story of the Church's Canon*. Peabody, MA: Hendrickson, 2012.

Moloney, Francis J., SDB. *Reading the New Testament in the Church: A Primer for Pastors, Religious Educators, and Believers*. Grand Rapids, MI: Baker Academic, 2015.

Senior, Donald, John J. Collins, Mary Ann Getty, eds. *The Catholic Study Bible*. 3rd ed. New York: Oxford University Press, 2016.

Witherup, Ronald D. *Scripture: Dei Verbum*. New York: Paulist Press, 2006.

———. *The Word of God at Vatican II: Exploring "Dei Verbum."* Collegeville, MN: Liturgical Press, 2014.

NOTES

NOTES

NOTES

NOTES